Folger Documents of Tudor and Stuart Civilization

THE ACTIONS OF THE
LOW COUNTRIES

FOLGER DOCUMENTS

OF TUDOR AND STUART CIVILIZATION

THIS volume is one of a series of publications of Tudor and Stuart documents that the Folger Library proposes to bring out. These documents will consist of hitherto unprinted manuscripts as well as reprints of rare books in the Folger Library. An effort will be made to choose significant items that will throw light on the social and intellectual background of the period from 1485 to 1715. In response to almost unanimous requests of interested historians, the spelling, punctuation, and capitalization will be modernized in printed texts. In some cases, where the original printing is clear and easily read, texts may be photographically reproduced. The Folger Library is prepared to supply microfilm of original texts to scholars who require a facsimile.

THE ACTIONS OF
THE LOW COUNTRIES

BY SIR ROGER WILLIAMS

EDITED BY

D. W. Davies

PUBLISHED FOR

The Folger Shakespeare Library

BY

CORNELL UNIVERSITY PRESS

Ithaca, New York

PREFACE

PROFESSOR W. Jappe Alberts, University of Utrecht, and Dr. D. Grosheide, University of Utrecht, have read the book in manuscript. They have corrected many grievous errors and improved the biographical sketches a very great deal. Mr. Jack Dunbar, Claremont Men's College, read all the notes and the biographical sketches. Mr. A. L. Rowse and Mr. John Gleason read the introduction and I am indebted to them for valuable suggestions and for correcting errors. I am also indebted for suggestions or assistance to Professor Pieter Geyl, University of Utrecht, Professor W. Ph. Coolhaas, University of Utrecht, Miss Mary Isabel Fry, Huntington Library, Mr. Louis B. Wright and his able staff at the Folger Shakespeare Library, and to Mr. Ian Philip of the Bodleian Library.

Mrs. Sumner James has typed the complete manuscript twice. The book could not have been prepared without her help. Mrs. Frederick L. Mulhauser modernized the punctuation in the text. I am also indebted for assistance to Mrs. Willem Swets, Miss Leonoor Swets, and Mr. Calvin de Pass.

The text follows the Folger Library copy of *The Actions of the Low Countries,* which is the first issue, but I want to thank Mrs. O. K. Wrigley of the Francis Bacon Library for permission to use that Library's copy of the second issue.

v

Preface

My wife has done a good deal of the proofreading and her help has been invaluable.

D. W. D.

Honnold Library
Claremont, California

CONTENTS

Contents

INTRODUCTION

THIS book is a firsthand account of the revolt in the Netherlands, the war which resulted eventually in Dutch independence. It was written by one of the most famous soldiers of the Elizabethan age, who took part in many of the battles he describes. Roger Williams fought for years in the Netherlands, and on both sides. He also took part in the English expedition to Portugal in 1589 and fought long in the French religious wars. He was known and liked by Henry IV of France, the Prince of Orange, the redoubtable Alessandro Farnese, Prince of Parma, and by many other French, Spanish, Dutch, and German generals. In England he numbered Walsingham, Leicester, and Essex among his friends and had a wide acquaintance among men of letters, politicians, and soldiers. Even Queen Elizabeth toward the end of her days acknowledged his worth and smiled kindly upon him. This eminence he achieved solely by his valor and skill as a soldier. He was born of a poor though ancient Welsh family of Penrhos in Monmouthshire. Like many another Welshman, he had to go among the English to make a living, but the story that he began life as a tailor seems highly unlikely. The picture of a man who would later be the imperious, impatient, hard-drinking, hard-fighting cavalry captain rubbing his hands obsequiously while a gentleman customer tried a new riding coat is a difficult one to conjure up. It is more reasonable to suppose that from his boyhood when he was

Introduction

a page to the Earl of Pembroke, who was himself a soldier, he continued to follow the wars throughout his lifetime. In 1572, when the events in the present narrative begin, he was about thirty-two years old and already a veteran, and he lived to enjoy another twenty-three years of almost continual fighting. It is also said that he spent some time at Oxford. If this is so, then probably those college years were also spent in fighting, merrymaking, and similar diversions, for Williams' books and letters give the impression that the unpretentious soldier and his pleasing style, direct, homely, and easy, escaped almost unscathed from the academic world.

His military career falls into two main periods, separated by two brief episodes. First, from 1572 through 1587, he fought in the Low Countries, either on the side of the Netherlanders or of the Spanish; second, from September, 1589, almost until the time of his death in 1595, he fought in the French religious wars. Between these two periods, in the years 1588 and 1589, he was a leading figure in the plans to repel the troops which the Spanish Armada expected to land in England, and following this he took part in the massive raid on Portugal in 1589. Throughout these combative years there was hardly a battle, a siege, a skirmish, a scuffle on a dike where if he were present his fearlessness and daring were not remarked by his friends or foes, sometimes by both. No matter how abused and neglected he felt, how disillusioned and disgusted he was with the Dutch, his commanders, or the English government, whether he had money and food or neither, when it came to fighting he distinguished himself. Soldiering was his trade, and he had an instinct for good workmanship.

The Low Countries, 1572–1587

Williams' activities in these years may be divided into three periods. First, from April, 1572, to December, 1573, he fought as a mercenary on the side of the rebelling Netherlanders against

Spain; second, in the four years from January, 1574, until December, 1577, he fought on the side of Spain against the Netherlanders; and third, in the period from August, 1578, to some time in 1587, he again fought for the Dutch, first as a mercenary in the army of the States-General and later in the English contingent sent by Queen Elizabeth to aid the Netherlanders. It should be hastily pointed out that Williams should not be criticized for fighting on both sides. Soldiers of fortune, genuine free lancers (Williams was a lancer by profession), were fighting throughout Europe wherever they could sell their skills. English, Scots, Walloons, Germans, and Dutch, for example, were fighting in the Spanish army in the Netherlands, and English, Scots, Walloons, Germans, and Dutch in the opposing army of Orange and the States-General. As Williams himself observes, a man went to war for any one of three reasons: money, honor, or duty. All three reasons were acceptable and respectable in his day; Williams usually fought for money.

His Netherlands adventure began in the spring of 1572. On April 1 of that year the momentous capture of Brielle occurred. Privateers with license from William of Orange took that city, and other towns quickly revolted from Spain or were captured by the Sea Beggars, as the privateers were called. The rebellious Netherlanders were meanwhile attempting to raise mercenary companies in England. This undertaking was made easier by the fact that unofficial intervention in the Netherlands was already a secret English policy. The English believed that this policy was the best method of forestalling French intervention and (later) of preventing Spain from securing possible invasion ports.

The first mercenary company, commanded by Thomas Morgan, arrived in Flushing before the month of April was over, and Williams was one of that company. The circumstances of the formation of the company are related by Williams in the present narrative. The English volunteers took part in the fighting in Zeeland until Morgan was replaced as commander by Sir Humphrey Gilbert, who undertook a more ambitious scheme. The brother of William the Silent, Ludwig of Nassau, had captured the city of Mons in the southern province of Hainaut and was besieged in the town by the forces of the Duke of Alva. Gilbert, with the English troops and some of the Flushingers, marched southward to relieve Ludwig. The expedition got as far south as Sluis, which was really not very far, and then attempted to capture that city. Being beaten off by the defenders, the English and Zeelanders retreated to Flushing. Williams relates his experiences on this excursion in the present volume.

When the proposed march to Mons came to nothing, the English next attempted to capture the town of Goes, not far from Flushing. They made two attempts to capture the city and both were miserable failures. The Flushingers indeed were so ashamed of this effort of their allies that they would not let them back into their city; and the English were so discouraged that Sir Humphrey Gilbert and his troops returned to England on November 5, 1572. Apparently Williams went home with his comrades, for he says in the present narrative

Our blow was so great [i.e., our defeat was so severe] that Sir Humphrey and the most of our men, not being acquainted with such disasters, sought all means to return into England. Notwithstanding, before we embarked, Sir William Morgan arrived from the Prince with authority from the Prince and the States in Holland to make large offers to stay Sir Humphrey and his regiment for their service, but all would not serve to stay either Sir Humphrey or any of his troops.

The defeat of the English troops made a deep impression on Williams. He spoke later of "our ignorant poor siege of Goes," and enlarged on how little the English knew of fighting at that period. He and his comrades got over the shock of defeat after being in England for a time, and during the siege of Haarlem ten English companies landed in the Netherlands, Williams among them.

In those days Haarlem was situated near the shores of a large lake or inland sea which has since been drained, the Haarlemmermeer. The forces of the States were able to get food and supplies into the besieged city across this lake by ship. On May 28, 1573, Williams and the English troops took part in a battle on the lake in which the ships of the Netherlanders were decisively defeated by the Spanish fleet. The Netherlanders having lost control of the water route, Haarlem was doomed, and it surrendered in mid-July. Williams remained in the neighborhood with the troops seeking to relieve the city until about the time it capitulated. He then took part in the capture of Gertruidenberg, was for a time garrisoned at Delft, and experienced further fighting in Zeeland. Unfortunately a quarrel developed between the Prince of Orange and Colonel Morgan, the commander of the English mercenaries. The English were discharged from the Prince's service, and by the beginning of January, 1574, Morgan and his men, Williams among them, were back in England. Williams was again unemployed.

Fortunately, unemployed English soldiers could generally be used in Ireland. Morgan and his men were ordered there, but Williams did not go with them. Instead, with four companions, he headed for Germany. Before the month was out he was no longer unemployed; he had become a soldier in the army of His Catholic Majesty Philip of Spain. How this came about he explains in the present narrative. "Most true it is," he says,

at Colonel Morgan's going into Ireland, hearing how the young Prince of Condé was newly escaped from France into Germany, meaning, as it was told me, to levy an army and to march with all speed into France, this bruit and my greedy desires to travel to see strange wars made me to quit the voyage into Ireland and to go with all speed toward the said Prince. Being arrived in Germany,

I found the Prince nothing ready to march, nor any speech of his sudden levy. Having spent there all the time I could, want of crowns forced me to return for England. Passing from Cologne toward Antwerp, and entering Lier in Brabant, I was brought before the master of the camp, Julián Romero, who . . . requested me earnestly to try his courtesy in the Spanish army, assuring me to depart when [it] pleased me. Having spent all my crowns, and being loath to return into England without seeing something, I promised to stay. . . . This was the manner and the first hour that I entered into the Spanish service.

Thus began the second period, the Spanish phase of Williams' fighting in the Netherlands. He entered the Spanish army before the end of January, 1574, and served his Iberian masters for four years. In his book, A *Brief Discourse of War* (1590), p. 29, he declares that he knew the Spanish army "by good experience, for I served under the ensigns of the *maestre de campo* Julián Romero twenty-two months, and Mondragón eighteen months, with the domestics of the brave Don John of Austria eight months, always in action. . . ." Williams joined the Spanish army, he says, because he did not want to return to England without seeing something. He got his wish. At the end of January, 1574, he was in the Battle of Reimerswaal on the Spanish side, and it was almost his last fight. The final action described in this book, it was a resounding defeat for the Spanish. "For my part," says Sir Roger, "I never saw anything so furious. . . . But for Julián Romero himself, I had been blown up with his *alférez* [his standard-bearer] yet I escaped with as great hazard as any other of his followers."

Williams' narrative breaks off here. At the time he was writing, probably in 1584, his fellow countrymen were thoroughly aroused to the danger which threatened them from Spain, and their days of peace were nearly over. They may not have taken kindly to a fellow countryman who had served Spain. Later, in 1590, after the Spanish had been thoroughly beaten, he wrote the second book already mentioned, *A Brief Discourse of War,* in which he described in detail the organization and customs of the Spanish army. He showed, too, a knowledge of Spanish troop dispositions in famous battles which an outsider could scarcely have had, but of actual participation in any Spanish campaign he wisely says nothing. Spain was still a touchy subject.

The forty months which Williams spent in the commands of Julián Romero and Cristobal Mondragón were not uneventful. They covered the period in which Don Luis de Requesens y Zuñiga had replaced the cruel and implacable Duke of Alva as Spanish commander in chief in the Netherlands. When, early in March, 1576, Requesens suddenly died, there was not a penny in the treasury. Lack of money and of a recognized leader brought about the collapse of the Spanish war effort. The unpaid Spanish troops mutinied and ruthlessly plundered the country. In desperation, representatives of the provinces met at Ghent on November 8, 1576, and signed an agreement in which they resolved to drive the Spanish soldiery from their country. The King of Spain sent his half brother, Don John of Austria, to replace Requesens and conciliate the provinces. Don John was entirely unsuccessful and ended by agreeing to remove the Spanish troops from the Low Countries. The troops actually left in April, 1577, and at that time Williams parted company with the Spanish army. He had completed the forty months of service with Romero and Mondragón of which he speaks, and he entered the household of the Governor, Don John of Austria, with whom, as he says, he served eight months, until December, 1577. During the months that Williams was with him the position of Don John had gotten steadily worse. The departure of the Spanish troops had deprived him of all authority and respect. The States-General and the Prince of Orange were now in control. By December, 1577, when Williams left his service, Don John had withdrawn to Luxembourg, on the fringe of the Netherlands. Powerless to fight or to rule, Don John had neither money nor employment for accomplished mercenary captains. The next action Williams saw was on the side of the States-General and the Prince of Orange.

The change from one side to the other apparently was not an easy one. Soon after Williams left the household of Don John, the relative positions of Spanish and Netherlanders were suddenly reversed. Three thousand Spanish troops returned to the Low Countries, and Alessandro Farnese, Prince of Parma, one of the greatest soldiers of the age, also arrived to assist Don John. At the Battle of Gembloux on February 1, 1578, the Spanish inflicted a crushing defeat on the Netherlanders. Town after town fell to the Spanish and considerable areas of the Low Countries were again at their mercy. The Prince of Orange and the States-General withdrew from Brussels to Antwerp and the fighting flared up with renewed vigor. Whilst Williams was still in the service of Don John, a new English contingent under the command of Sir John Norris had arrived in the Netherlands (July, 1577) to enter the service of the States-General. Williams, who had returned to England after leaving Don John, now sought to join Norris' contingent. Both Leicester and Walsingham wrote letters in his behalf to William Davison, the Queen's agent in the Low Countries. Walsingham asked Davison to intercede for Williams with the Prince of Orange. Leicester prayed that Davison himself would forget the unfavorable opinion he had formed of Williams and endeavor to have the Welsh captain reinstated in the Prince's favor. "Pray let me entreat you," he wrote, "that the valor of the man, who is indeed a very good soldier, may overweight with you to private offense, and that you will remit it and deal in his favor with the Prince and others."[1] Neither Davison nor the Prince was to be easily induced to take a favorable view of Williams. Davison

[1] *Calendar of State Papers, Foreign, 1577–1578*, p. 693, Leicester to Davison, May 17, 1578.

had been in the Low Countries for a number of years, and the Prince had a thorough knowledge of what had transpired in his country. Probably both were very well acquainted with Williams' services for Spain.

Finally Leicester and Walsingham prevailed and Williams was given a commission in Norris' regiment. Once re-established, he quickly gained the admiration and respect of all, for he was, as Leicester had said, "indeed a very good soldier." He became Norris' chief lieutenant and was on intimate terms with the Prince of Orange. "In all our journeys," Norris wrote to Walsingham at the beginning of 1581, "no man has won honor near to Captain Williams, both in our own camp and in the enemy's." [2] Later in the same year the Prince of Orange also assured Walsingham that ever since Williams had been with him he had acted "like a man of honor in all warlike encounters and actions." [3]

Williams' actions in 1581 and 1582 can be glimpsed in his letters to Walsingham and others. He fought for a time in Friesland and Gelderland. He returned home to England briefly, then spent some time at Antwerp, and later was at Bruges. These were difficult years for the Netherlanders, for Parma was a better general than any of his opponents, and the Spanish troops were the best in Europe. In these trying circumstances the army of the States-General was discouraged and discontented. The morale of the English troops reached a low ebb in the summer of 1582. The troops were as usual unpaid. A rumor circulated that Sir John Norris had received three months' pay for the regiment and had kept the money for himself. The English mutinied and were held in the camp at Dunkirk with the greatest difficulty, and Norris fumed with indignation. "If any man can prove," he exclaimed, "that since I came into this country I have stayed from any captain or soldier the value of one stiver

[2] *CSP, For., 1581–1582*, p. 75, February 26, 1581.
[3] *Ibid.*, p. 370, Prince of Orange to Walsingham, November 15, 1581.

of his due, I am content to be accounted the veriest villain of the world." [4] The sad state of affairs was reported to Walsingham by Colonel Thomas Morgan. "In my opinion," he wrote, "there was never a greater disorder or discredit to our nation than has fallen out at this time. The soldiers exclaim on the general [Norris]; the general finds fault with the captain, but whose the fault is I know not." [5] One of the most outspoken in his criticism of Norris was Williams. He admitted he owed a great deal to the general. He had been the first captain chosen by Norris, but Norris could not say it was he who had taught Williams to be a soldier. Williams was offered a commission in the French contingent and was tempted to take it.

While the internal wrangling continued, there were skirmishes with Parma's army. Williams captured the colors of a troop of enemy cavalry, and an enemy raid on the camp was repulsed because "Captain Williams and Captain Yorke showed themselves so valiant." [6] The troops moved from Dunkirk to Bruges and from Bruges to Ghent, still wrangling. An observer reported that the common English soldiers were miserable from continual marching and lack of money and food. Their officers, he thought, were envious of one another; intent on getting what they could for themselves, they acted generally like a pack of hirelings. Williams, he said, "either by enticement of others or fantasticalness of himself . . . has of late withdrawn himself and his company of horse from the rest of our English and joined himself to the French after the example of Rowland Yorke and Mr. Cotton." [7] Finally, at Bruges in mid-August, Norris gathered his officers together, had a frank discussion with them, and satisfied them that he had not withheld their pay. The States-General, alarmed at these developments, hastened to pay the

[4] *CSP, For., 1582*, p. 223, Norris to Walsingham, August 5, 1582.
[5] *Ibid.*, p. 191, July 27, 1582.
[6] *Ibid.*, p. 220, Cobham to Burghley, August 4, 1582.
[7] *Ibid.*, p. 273, Knollys to Walsingham, August 24, 1582.

troops. Meanwhile the English regiment attended when necessary to the grim business of fighting. In the first days of September an all-day battle was fought near the walls of Ghent, and,
of all the troops engaged, the English behaved best. Williams
was the only cavalry commander who volunteered to charge
the enemy.[8] By December, Williams and Norris were completely
reconciled, and the former wrote to Walsingham that Norris
"does now favor me as he had done heretofore." [9]

During the spring and summer of 1583, Norris was in England,
and during his absence Williams commanded his regiment. He
found the responsibility arduous. The troops were again unpaid,
they were deserting, and Williams desired nothing so much as
the return of his general. "For God's sake make haste," [10] he
implored Norris. Two days later he repeated the plea. "It is
more than time you were here," he chided; "I pray make all
speed you can. . . . You shall find great change. If I would
endure this life for any time for any gage [i.e., pay], I am no
honest man. I am sure this nine days I have not slept forty
hours." [11]

At this time Williams was contending not only with a vigilant
enemy before him and neglectful employers behind him but
also with what amounted to a separatist movement if not treason
in the nearby city of Ghent. That city a few years before had
been under the control of a party of extreme Calvinists. The
citizens were so anxious not to fall again into the power of these
fanatics that they held secret negotiations with the Prince of
Parma, and many said openly that they wanted nothing more
to do with the Prince of Orange. In October, 1583, Williams
was garrisoned in the town of Aalst. The leaders in Ghent
plotted to gain control of Aalst and to sell out the city to Parma.

[8] *Ibid.*, p. 296, Herle to Walsingham, September 1/2, 1582.
[9] *Ibid.*, p. 504, Williams to Walsingham, December 15, 1582.
[10] *CSP, For.*, 1583–1584, p. 27, July 18/28, 1583.
[11] *Ibid.*, p. 30, July 20/30, 1583.

Introduction

As part of the plot, traitorous Walloons in Williams' command were to yield a gate of the town to troops from Ghent who were then on the march to Aalst. Williams discovered the plot just in time and removed the traitorous troops. The very people the English were supposedly aiding, he wrote, now sought by "all the means possible to defeat us. Our case is poor and miserable. We have served them long, honestly, with valor, as the world does know. They owe us at the least 200,000 crowns or better. To be quit of us they seek all means possible to cut our throats." [12]

Having failed to get control of Aalst by bribing the Gantois, Parma then offered bribes to Williams. The Welsh soldier refused,[13] but Parma was to succeed with others less ruggedly honest. The English troops had been unpaid for months and were even without food. "The sergeant major with the captains and a number of officers came to my lodging," wrote Williams. "[They] told me resolutely to get me out of the town . . . and not to return without money." [14] On these orders from his erstwhile comrades, Williams departed. He laid the desperate case of the English in Aalst before the Prince and the States-General, but the governmental machinery ground very slowly. Meanwhile, in Aalst the desperate English captains tried without success to obtain contributions of food and money from neighboring cities. In reply to their pleas, the people of Ghent, for example, declared they could spare nothing for Aalst. In fact they devoutly wished "the town were afire and all you bound fast in the midst." [15] In desperation the English captains finally sold out the town to the Prince of Parma. Williams was profoundly discouraged. "Your Honor does counsel me," he

[12] *Ibid.*, p. 124, Williams to Walsingham, October 12, 1583.

[13] *CSP, For., 1584–1585*, p. 51, Williams to Walsingham, September 4, 1584.

[14] *CSP, For., 1583–1584*, p. 240, Williams to Walsingham, November 27/ December 7, 1583.

[15] *Ibid.*

wrote Walsingham, "to stay here in any honest sort rather than spend my time idly in England. God knows my misery is great and like not to be remedied in staying." [16]

He stayed, however, and in March, 1584, he was attached to German troops fighting in Gelderland. He expected nothing commendable of Germans, and on this occasion the behavior of his companions confirmed his low opinion. The opposing troops were under the command of Nicolao Basta, and, Williams wrote Walsingham, if it had not been that he had a company of cowards on his own side, Basta would have been thoroughly basted in short order. "Every man," he remarked with heavy-handed sarcasm, "was valiant by reason the river was betwixt us [and the enemy]." [17] Fortunately, his association with his German companions was not of long duration. Welsh and Germans probably fight better separately, and even better when on opposite sides.

Later in this same year, 1584, Williams was involved in a skirmish at Zutphen. Some of his troopers became embroiled with the Spanish under De Taxis (or De Tassis). The fight was unimportant except as it indicates that war was a more sporting proposition in those days. Williams got the worst of the encounter, and two of his men were taken prisoner. He sent a trumpeter to De Taxis offering to ransom his soldiers and gave an alibi for having lost. "I hope," he wrote De Taxis, "your horsemen will not make too much of this skirmish, for I swear to you on the faith of a gentleman and a soldier, I had in all only nineteen lances and eleven harquebusiers." He concluded, "Yours affectionate to serve you, saving the cause of quarrel." [18] De Taxis returned the prisoners and remarked: "As to the skirmish yesterday, I had mounted my horse to see the sport between yours and ours, but your retreat was so hasty that we

---

[16] *Ibid.*, p. 309, January 16/26, 1583.
[17] *Ibid.*, pp. 429–430, March 24, 1584.
[18] *Ibid.*, p. 555, June 11, 1584.

had not the pleasure. Yours affectionately to serve you, saving the cause of quarrel, De Taxis." [19]

In the midst of such fighting and skirmishing occurred a truly significant event, the assassination of the Prince of Orange. In July of 1584 the Prince was at Delft, and Williams happened to be there with him. The circumstances of the murder of the Prince have often been related. The murderer was in the entrance hall as the Prince and his wife went into the dining room for lunch. The Prince dined with his family and one guest, a visiting burgomaster. After lunch the Prince spoke briefly to two officers in the dining room, Colonel Morgan and an Italian officer. As he left the dining room he spoke to Roger Williams, who had dropped to one knee. The Prince laid his hand on Williams' head as he passed. Almost immediately the murderer, Balthasar Gérard, fired at the Prince at close range, wounding him mortally, and fled. It is usually said that Gérard was caught by a lackey and a halberdier. An account sent home to England four days after the murder says that Gérard was taken, as he sought to climb the wall, by Captain Williams with a boy and several others. If this account is correct, Williams ran true to form. Whenever a situation required decisiveness and courage, he was in the forefront.

In the fall of the year, after the death of the Prince, Williams was back in England, and indeed was writing the present book. At the beginning of the next year, 1585, he was in France, but by the summer he had returned to the Low Countries. It was in 1585 that Queen Elizabeth brought herself to help openly the rebelling Netherlanders. The period of surreptitious aid was over, and England became the open ally of the Netherlanders. She began negotiations to render aid in November, 1584, but it was not until August 2, 1585, that a treaty was signed. It was agreed that Brielle, Flushing, and the fort of Rammekens, not far from Flushing, were to be turned over by the Dutch to

[19] *Ibid.*, De Taxis to Williams, June 11, 1584.

the English, to be held until the costs of the English expeditionary force which Elizabeth was sending were repaid. In August,
1585, the very month in which the treaty was signed, Williams
asked for a commission in the new English forces. "So do I
humbly desire Your Majesty," he wrote, "to give me the place
of lieutenant of the cavalry if Your Highness thinks me worthy.
I have commanded divers times a squadron of lancers afore
the enemies. I trust neither they nor friends can prove that
ever I received any disgrace hitherunto." [20] Part, at least, of
the request was granted. Williams was commissioned in the
English forces, but in the infantry rather than the cavalry.

By September, 1585, although the commander in chief, the
Earl of Leicester, had not arrived, there were twenty-three
companies of English in the Netherlands, equipped and paid
by Queen Elizabeth. Some of the companies constituted an
English contingent. Other companies were attached to the Dutch
forces. Williams was placed in command of a number of the
companies and given a difficult assignment. There were indica-
tions that some civic leaders in Bergen-op-Zoom intended to
betray the city to the Spanish. Williams was sent into the town
with eight companies of English infantry to hold it for the
States-General. The town governor at the time was Bartholomew
Balfour, a well-known Scottish captain, who was anti-English.
The Walloon troops under his command were pro-Spanish. The
situation was perilous, but Williams mixed the Walloons with
his English soldiers so that in each company guarding the walls
the English outnumbered Walloons. In describing his actions
to Sir Philip Sidney, Williams wrote, "I know not in whose
pay I am, but I am sure if there be any place of danger or
of disgrace to be acquainted with it." [21] Certainly, his dealings
with Balfour and the traitorous Walloons within the town and
his skirmishing with the enemy without provided enough action

[20] *CSP, For., 1584–1585*, p. 687, Williams to the Queen, August 31, 1585.
[21] *CSP, For., 1585–1586*, p. 51, September 30, 1585.

to satisfy even Williams, but it still grieved him "to be on foot and to see the enemies braving on horseback. . . . True it is I have great pay on foot. I had rather take half on horseback. . . ."[22]

Perhaps he never gained more glory than he did in these years. On the one hand, the States' army was stronger and the English more numerous, and on the other hand, the Prince of Parma saw to it that his opponents had few dull moments. Best of all, perhaps, Williams was fighting under a commander, Leicester, whom at this time he respected and who in turn valued the Welsh soldier highly. "Roger Williams is worth his weight in gold," Leicester reported, "for he is no more valiant than he is wise and of judgment to govern his doings."[23] One of his more daring actions in this period was a raid with Marten Schenk, another valorous commander, on Parma's army, which was besieging the friendly town of Venlo. The Prince of Orange ordered Schenk and Williams to attempt to fight their way through the Spanish army and to enter Venlo. The two men commanded 800 infantry and 600 cavalry, 120 of the latter being English. Ordered to get into Venlo if possible, the expedition marched day and night until it arrived near the city. Schenk and Williams decided to leave the infantry behind and to attempt to knife through the Spanish army with the cavalry alone. Unfortunately, the German horsemen had no enthusiasm for the proposed adventure, and the two leaders proceeded to tackle the army of Spain with a force of 150 lancers, comprising the 120 English and 30 Germans. They attacked the Spanish camp at midnight and achieved complete surprise, actually hacking their way to Parma's tent and there killing some of his grenadiers and his secretary. They then attempted to force their way to the gates of Venlo, but the Spanish had concentrated strong

[22] *Ibid.,* pp. 70–71, Williams to Walsingham, October 8, 1585.
[23] *Correspondence of Robert Dudley, Earl of Leicester, during His Government of the Low Countries,* ed. James Bruce (London, 1844), p. 430.

forces around the gates and repelled all their attacks. The fighting continued from midnight until daybreak. By that time the whole Spanish army was aroused and in arms, and Schenk and Williams beat a retreat with Parma's cavalry corps in pursuit. Of the 150 horsemen in the attacking party, between 30 and 40 were killed or taken prisoner.[24] This was one of the more daring cavalry raids, but not the only one performed by Williams in these months. Le Petit, a historian of the war, notes that Williams and Count Hohenlohe also raided into Brabant and pillaged Langstraat.

In September, 1586, at the siege of Duisburg, Williams received one of his many wounds. "Roger Williams," wrote Leicester, "hath got a blow through the arm. . . . I warned him of it, being in trench with me, . . . [but he] would need run up and down so oft out of the trench, with a great plume of feathers in his gilt morion, as, so many shot coming at him, he could hardly escape with so little hurt." [25]

When Leicester went to the Netherlands, Queen Elizabeth had granted him the power to confer knighthoods. The Queen herself exercised this function with the greatest parsimony, but Leicester was made of more generous stuff. In October, 1586, he gathered together a group of soldiers who had distinguished themselves, including Williams, and knighted them. It was fortunate the honor came to Williams when it did, for in the following month Leicester was recalled to England. He had been sent to the Netherlands as commander of the English forces and had arrived there in December, 1585. On New Year's Day, 1586, the Dutch had offered him the office of Governor of the Netherlands, and he had accepted. His acceptance was a very great political blunder, and Queen Elizabeth was furious with him. Leicester also proved himself an unskillful general,

---

[24] *CSP, For., 1586–1587*, pp. 19–20, Lord North to Burghley, June 16, 1586.

[25] *Correspondence of Robert Dudley*, p. 407.

and by the time of his recall the Netherlanders were thoroughly disillusioned.

Ten months after receiving his knighthood Williams himself also suffered a reversal of fortune. He had commanded the English defenders of the town of Sluis when it surrendered to the besieging Spanish army under Parma. The loss of Sluis was regarded as a calamity, since Parma could use the town as a port of embarkation for the invasion of England. It was also one of the bitterest experiences of Williams' life. Sir Roger had been originally ordered to Ostend, but when it became obvious that Parma was bent on taking Sluis, Williams thrust himself into the town with five companies and also brought in supplies for the defenders. The Spanish siege began early in June and lasted sixty days. The defenders, Williams says in his account of the siege, numbered slightly less than sixteen hundred fighting men and pioneers combined. With these they had to guard two and a half miles of defenses and two forts. On July 8, he relates, they were battered with thirty cannon and eight culverins from three o'clock in the morning until five in the evening, the Spanish firing into the town more than four thousand cannon shot. The Prince of Parma himself later declared that he had never seen such furious cannonading. A breach was made in the wall about 250 yards in length. Five times during the day the Spanish assaulted the breach. Each time there was desperate hand-to-hand fighting. Each time the Spanish were thrown back.

After this harrowing experience, the defenders held the town for another eighteen days. The Spanish gained possession of the breach in the wall and stretches of the wall itself. During these last eighteen days, relates Williams, his troops fought with pikes, pistols, swords, and stones to hold the town. One Spanish assault on the defending lines lasted from nine in the morning until two in the afternoon. For the last nine days the

Spanish attacks came almost hourly. The enemy was so far into the ramparts that their volleys enfiladed the defenders. From time to time Williams managed to send a letter to England through the besieging forces, describing the situation and pleading desperately for help. "We have not now powder for three skirmishes," he wrote Walsingham on July 18; "For myself I wish myself dead for debauching so many brave men unto their ruin. . . . The old saying is true, wit is never good until it be dearly bought, but I and the rest of my companions have and is like to pay too dear for it." [26] For the last eighteen days of the siege the English ate and slept in their combat positions. Of twenty cannon in the town at the beginning of the siege, four were working when it ended. Of the original sixteen hundred defenders, English, Flemings, and Walloons, Williams says, not seven hundred marched out when the town capitulated.

Williams remained very bitter about the loss of Sluis. Four days after the surrender he was feeling so badly that he declared himself ready to follow Lady Walsingham's advice to quit the wars and marry a merchant's widow.[27] He felt that his command had been sacrificed and forsaken. Leicester, who supposedly was to come to his aid, re-embarked his troops without a fight, and a coolness developed between the men afterward. "I speak this for the wrongs done unto myself and companions for the defense of the town of Sluis," wrote Williams.

True it is, those that serves many, serves nobody. I mean they shall find none that will confess to be their masters, especially when they should be rewarded for their service; but the multitude will be ready to disgrace their servants, thinking by such means to pay them their debts.[28]

[26] *CSP, For., 1587,* p. 184, July 18, 1587.
[27] *Ibid.,* p. 210, Williams to Walsingham, July 30, 1587.
[28] *A Brief Discourse of War* (1590), p. 54.

Introduction

The defense against the Spanish Armada and the expedition to Portugal

Sluis fell at the end of July, 1587, and by December of that year Williams was back in England, as were many others who had earned their bread fighting in France and the Low Countries. The Invincible Armada was gathering in the ports of Spain, and all good Englishmen stood by to repel invasion. That for which Williams had often vainly petitioned, a place in the forces of his own country, was now his. In December, 1587, he was sent to Wales, one of a number of captains who went into various parts of the realm to examine the state of the forces. In the following March he was one of a group of military leaders planning the defenses against the Spanish invasion. The group decided which ports to fortify and the desirable proportions of pikemen, harquebusiers, and cavalry in the forces, and attempted to guess the probable Spanish landing beaches. By June, Williams was not with the army but with the fleet, as an adviser on troop landings. As Lord Howard, the fleet commander, explained to Walsingham, he had chosen Sir Roger Williams "for his experience by land, what occasion soever might fall out to land in Ireland or Scotland or in England; for, God willing, if it please God to send us wind to serve us, we mean to land some with them wheresoever they land in any of Her Majesty's dominions." [29]

Meanwhile, an army of four thousand was gathered together to repel the expected invasion, and Leicester, the commander in chief, asked for Williams as commander of the lancers.[30] The troops were encamped at Tilbury, where there was a dearth

[29] *Defeat of the Spanish Armada,* ed. John Knox Laughton (London, 1894), I, 210.

[30] *The Manuscripts of the Right Honorable F. J. Savile Foljambe of Osberton. Historical Manuscripts Commission Report XV Append., Pt. V* (London, 1897), 52.

of provisions and munitions and an acute shortage of officers. Despite this shortage of competent commanders, when the Spanish Armada was off Plymouth, both Norris and Williams hurried to Dover. If the Spanish landed they wanted to be there, but meanwhile Leicester was fuming at Tilbury. "I assure you, I am angry with Sir John Norris and Sir Roger Williams," he wrote Walsingham; "They were both appointed by mine own desire, as well as otherwise to offices of great charge, Mr. Norris as marshal of our companies, the other of the horsemen." [31] Fortunately he was soon able to report that the two had returned, adding, "In the meanwhile they have put me to more travail than ever I was in before." [32]

There was, of course, no invasion, and with the defeat of the Armada the army at Tilbury was broken up. In October both Norris and Williams were back in the Low Countries, and in the following month Williams returned home with dispatches.[33] At the time he returned an exciting adventure was brewing, one he could not resist. The English answer to the Spanish Armada was to be a massive land and sea operation against Portugal. Don Antonio, Prior of Crato, the pretender to the crown of Portugal, had assured Queen Elizabeth that if he were landed in Portugal with a small force the people would flock to his standard and throw off the yoke of Spain. The proposal to invade Portugal was attractive to the Queen and her ministers. It made sense politically and offered an opportunity for booty. During the winter of 1588–1589 the expedition was assembled at Plymouth, partly private venture, partly government undertaking.

[31] *CSP, Domestic, 1581–1590*, p. 511, Leicester to Walsingham, July 25, 1588; *Defeat of the Spanish Armada*, I, 306.

[32] *Ibid.*, I, 321.

[33] Lady Georgina Bertie, *Five Generations of a Loyal House*, I, 224–226, as quoted by J. Dover Wilson, "Martin Marprelate and Shakespeare's Fluellen: A New Theory of the Authorship of the Marprelate Tracts," *The Library*, 3rd. ser., III (London, 1912), 127.

One other could not resist the expedition, Williams' friend and the Queen's favorite, the Earl of Essex. Twenty-six ships and eleven thousand soldiers were ready to sail from Plymouth, but Essex was forbidden by Elizabeth to be one of that martial company, a circumstance which, as it turned out, was unlucky for Williams. Essex, secure in the belief that the Queen would not punish him too severely, appropriated a royal ship, the "Swiftsure," and accompanied by Williams sailed from Falmouth at the same time the rest of the expedition sailed from Plymouth. There can be no doubt it was Essex who purloined the Queen's ship. Only he had the prestige so to overawe both officers and crew that they obeyed his orders; but the Queen preferred to blame Williams. She sent a hasty message to Drake and Norris, the commanders of the expedition. She did not doubt but that they had thoroughly weighed the heinousness of the offense lately committed by Sir Roger Williams in forsaking the army with one of the Queen's ships. If they had not already inflicted the death penalty, they were to deprive Williams of his command and place him under arrest. They would disregard her commands at their own peril. As a matter of fact, she may have suspected that her wishes would be disregarded. Walsingham was even averse to sending the letter. Williams, he pointed out, was beloved throughout the army. If he were punished as the Queen directed, the resulting discontent might endanger the success of the expedition.

Actually, the expedition was unsuccessful anyway, for, contrary to prognostications, the Portuguese did not rally to Don Antonio. The English plundered and burned Corunna. Norris' troops landed at Peniche and marched overland to Lisbon. The fleet under Drake ascended the Tagus to cooperate with the land forces in the capture of Lisbon. The army wore itself out in marching overland from Peniche and there was little effective cooperation between sea and land forces. Needless to say, Lisbon was not taken. It was some consolation that when the English

troops faced their adversaries in open field, they proved themselves superior. The troops whom Williams fought earned only
his contempt. "The world doth know," he wrote,

> five thousand of our nation made guards at the gates of Lisbon
> four days, although there were in the town five thousand Spaniards,
> four thousand Portuguese carrying arms; besides they were assured
> of all the burgesses. . . . Also the world knows we were not set
> out with our sovereign's royal forces; notwithstanding, we gave them
> the law thirty days in their countries.[34]

Eventually the English had to withdraw, with Essex and
Williams fighting rear-guard actions until the troops were re-
embarked for England. Later Williams wrote Walsingham that
twelve thousand foot and a thousand lancers could march
through Spain and Portugal and dictate a peace on their own
terms.[35] The statement appears too sanguine; but Sir Roger
was always optimistic about English troops, especially if he
led them, and, to be fair, his expectations were usually justified.

The expedition returned home having accomplished very
little, and Williams personally had marred his fortunes by in-
curring the Queen's displeasure. His departure with Essex in
the "Swiftsure" had led Elizabeth to view him as an irresponsible,
vainglorious old soldier, no fit companion for the young Earl.

The French period

Almost immediately after the raid on Portugal, Williams became involved in the war in France. For many years there
had been civil war in that country between the Huguenots, led
by Henry of Navarre, and the Catholic party, led by Navarre's
predecessors on the French throne and by the powerful family
of Guise. In July, 1589, Henry of Navarre was crowned King
of France, but the desperate struggle with the Catholic party,

---

[34] *A Brief Discourse of War*, pp. 8–9.
[35] *CSP, Domestic, 1581–1590*, p. 603, June 1, 1589.

which was supported by Spain, gave no sign of ending. The answer to Spanish intervention was an English expedition to aid the Huguenots. An army was formed in England to go to the aid of the French king. The commander was Peregrine Bertie, Lord Willoughby, and Williams was one of his lieutenants. The expedition arrived in France in September, 1589, and Williams soon distinguished himself at the siege of Paris. While the city was being assailed by the forces of Henry of Navarre, the Catholic Leaguers got between the besieging army and the Channel coast and thus cut off Willoughby's communication with England. In this situation Willoughby found, as he informed Queen Elizabeth, that the only man who could be relied upon to get through with dispatches was Sir Roger.

Williams had not been pardoned by the Queen for his part in the "Swiftsure" incident and had been under the cloud of her displeasure since the return of the Portuguese expedition. In May, 1590, he wrote to the Lord Treasurer humbly craving the favor "to obtain my sovereign's passport to depart out of her realm." He protested that he loved Her Majesty, and ventured to say that "Her Highness' greatest enemies cannot deny but I am one that deserved better news. Her Majesty forgave many offenders. I persuade myself venturing my life so often, as I did, deserved pardon, offending no more than I did." He believed that if he were allowed to go abroad, his behavior "has not been so ill but to be welcome into the most places." [36] But if he were not allowed to fight, he could at least write, and this he did. It was in this year that he published his *Brief Discourse of War*. He probably obtained his passport the same month in which he petitioned for it, for before the end of May he was present at a conference outside Paris between Henry of Navarre and the representatives of the League.

[36] British Museum, Dept. of MSS. Catalogue Harl. 6995. Original letters of State, warrants, etc., (f 30-b) 1590–1592. Williams to the Lord Treasurer, May 2, 1590.

In the following year an English expeditionary force commanded by Essex was sent to the aid of the French king. Specifically the expedition was to aid in the capture of Rouen, which was held by Henry IV's enemies, the Catholic Leaguers. The project had been poorly planned, and the English force had been hastily put together. Sir Thomas Wilkes, a prominent diplomat and soldier, remarked, "Sir Thomas Shirley and myself were appointed counselors to the Earl, which with much ado we have avoided (as I hope); and I have not known so gallant a troop go out of England with so many young and untrained commanders." [37] This force under Essex had been preceded by one of 3,000 men under Sir John Norris, which had been dispatched to France in May, 1591, and which had included Sir Roger Williams. Norris' force was destined to succor the King's forces fighting in Brittany, but a detachment of 600 men under Williams was sent to Dieppe to keep the port open for further reinforcements. Consequently, when Essex with his 3,600 men reached Dieppe, he was met by Williams, who became marshal of the newly arrived force. Indeed, Williams acted not only as marshal of the army but also, since he knew the King and the language of the country, as liaison officer between Essex and Henry IV of France. The office of marshal was analogous to executive officer to the commander in chief. As Williams himself wrote, "The office of the marshal is painful and great, for he meddleth with the whole affairs of the wars." [38]

Glimpses of Williams performing his task as marshal are given by Sir Thomas Coningsby, who kept a journal of the expedition. Under the date of August 15, 1591, Coningsby notes that by six in the morning they were on horseback and that they were put in good order by the marshal before beginning the day's march. A few days later Williams took an action

[37] Sir Thomas Coningsby, "Journal of the Siege of Rouen, 1591," in *The Camden Miscellany* (London, 1847), p. 8.
[38] *A Brief Discourse of War*, p. 16.

which was characteristic of him. When the advance scouts sighted a large body of unidentified troops, Williams, although second in command in the army, rode forward himself until he was satisfied these were enemy formations. About a week later he discovered about 240 enemy cavalry hovering on the flank of the column. Calling upon the Earl of Essex to take direct command of the forces, he placed himself at the head of the lancers, and, says Coningsby, all day long he kept the enemy in view and his lancers ready to fight.[39]

By the beginning of October the forces of Navarre and his English allies were before Rouen, but the Leaguers were in sure possession of it. The besiegers had done very little, since they had no siege artillery. The English expedition, costing money every day, had now been gone more than two months. Elizabeth was completely exasperated. "We declared our pleasure to be that both you and our forces should return after the end of the two months," she wrote Essex on October 4,

according as was accorded afore your going thither, and having showed and sent you very good causes which moved us thereto, such as if you had well weighed them with a mind and judgment not blinded with vain persuasions, either of yourself or of such others as do accompany you with their glorious windy discourses, you would have readily assented thereto.[40]

It is not difficult to guess which one of Essex' companions Elizabeth considered to be full of glorious windy discourses, for she continued by remarking that she had condemned a previous attempt on Rouen for its rashness, and yet despite her censure and that of others Roger Williams had persisted in an audacious and foolish manner to extol the action and thus had revealed the fact that he had been the author of the plan. Having done one foolish thing, the Queen continued, he might well do others.

[39] Coningsby, "Journal," pp. 13, 19.
[40] *Hist. MSS Com., Salisbury MSS, Pt. IV*, pp. 143–144, October 4, 1591.

Considering he has the principal office of the field as marshal, and thereby, and by the credit he presumes to have with you, our general, we do think it very convenient to avoid all such occasions by his dangerous advices, and therefore we will and command you that no action of any moment be attempted by his advice, either privately or publicly, without the assent of Sir Thomas Leighton and some other of the captains of most discretion and understanding.

It must be admitted that Williams, a man of imagination, saw more opportunities for action than the Queen had authorized. Arriving at Caudebec, a town a short distance down river from Rouen, he wrote Essex that had the army marched to Caudebec "when we thought once to have done, . . . we had taken it within two days." [41] Possession of Caudebec would have enabled the English to cut off supplies going up river to Rouen, but what would have been the wrath of Elizabeth if, persuaded by Williams, Essex had attempted not only the capture of Rouen but of Caudebec also?

Not only were the besiegers without siege artillery, but their troops were too few, the town strong, and its commander resolute. There were the usual skirmishes, surprise attacks, and sorties. On December 6 the defenders sallied in force and caused panic among the besiegers. "You never saw such running," wrote Coningsby, "and had it not been for Sir Roger Williams, Sir Thomas Baskerville, Sir Thomas Gerrard, myself and others, I think they had run till this time. . . ." [42]

In January, 1592, Essex was recalled, and three months later, Parma, raiding southward from the Netherlands with a strong force, broke up the siege. By June, Roger Williams was back in England, for on the nineteenth of that month he made his will.[43]

In the following years Williams fought for the French king

[41] *Ibid.*, p. 148, October 20, 1591.   [42] Coningsby, "Journal," p. 58.
[43] *Hist. MSS Com. Report V, Pt. I*, p. 266. In *HMC, Salisbury Papers, Addenda, Pt. XIII*, p. 414, there is another will dated June 19, 1589.

in Normandy, and many events indicated the esteem and respect which Henry of Navarre had for him. In 1594 the King employed him to carry dispatches to Essex, the Queen, and others, and on one occasion called his great merits to the attention of the Queen, adding "not that you were not sufficiently acquainted with them already and that I have not before given you proofs of his worth on several occasions." [44] One's impression from reading the correspondence of various persons is that the French king looked upon Williams with affection and respect.

By 1595 Williams was well known in the Netherlands, in France, in England, and doubtless in Spain also. Even the Queen was now gracious to him. On July 26, Anthony Standen, one of England's secret agents, noted in a letter to Anthony Bacon, the brother of Francis Bacon: "Sir Roger [Williams] hath this night in presence of all the court received of Her Majesty a friendly public welcome." [45] On September 2, the same writer, again at the court, wrote that Sir Roger Williams was with the Queen and that she was "dispatching [him] to the French king wherever he be." [46]

Williams had proved his worth and attained fame, but he did not live long to enjoy it. A correspondent wrote to Sir Robert Sidney, brother of Sir Philip Sidney, on December 8, 1595: "Sir Roger Williams hath been dangerously sick of a hot burning ague that came by a surfeit, but is a very little better." [47] Five days later, December 13, 1595, the same correspondent again wrote to Robert Sidney to announce that

Sir Roger Williams died of a surfeit in B[aynard's?] Castle yesterday at three o'clock after midnight. He gave all he had to my Lord of Essex who, indeed, saved his soul, for none but he could make him

[44] *Hist. MSS Com., Salisbury MSS, Pt. IV*, p. 549, June 10/20, 1594.

[45] Thomas Birch, *Memoirs of the Reign of Queen Elizabeth* (London, 1754), I, 269.

[46] *Ibid.*, 294.

[47] Arthur Collins, *Letters and Memorials of State* (London, 1746), I, 375.

take a feeling of his end; but he died well and very repentant. His jewels are valued at £1,000. 'Tis said he had £1,200 out at interest. In ready gold he had £200 and £60 in silver. His plate is worth £60, his garments £30, his horses £60, and this is his end. He desires to be buried in Powles [i.e., St. Paul's], and I hear my Lord of Essex means to have it done in very good martial sort.[48]

Williams' death was widely lamented. It was said that the Scottish king "wished he had lost five thousand of his own people for his life, and intended to write his epitaph."[49] Robert Beale, who had been with Leicester in the attempt to relieve Sluis, wrote to Sir Robert Sidney, December 21, 1595: "The deaths of your noble uncle, the Earl of Huntingdon, Dr. Whittakers in Cambridge, and Sir Roger Williams here, all three worthy men in their calling and hardly to be seconded again, portend some scourge upon us for the multitude of our sins and transgressions."[50] On December 22 another correspondent wrote: "Tomorrow Sir Roger Williams is buried, and I fear Sir Thomas Morgan will die this night."[51] So ended the days of a brave soldier and an able commander.

The character and reputation of Sir Roger Williams

From the numerous letters of Williams and his friends, and from the two books and part of another which he wrote, a clear impression of the man emerges. He was by trade a soldier and as such he ought to be primarily judged. He was valorous beyond question. In the surviving letters and documents no instance appears in which he acted less bravely than one would wish. Indeed, one can almost say that on every occasion he was braver, more decisive, and more resolute than could be expected. As commander of a troop of horse or of a regiment he was excellent. One may have some doubts about his performance in command of larger units; the alacrity with which he acted as

[48] *Ibid.*, 377.
[50] Collins, I, 396.

[49] *Birch*, I, 355.
[51] *Ibid.*, 384.

scout and cavalry captain when actually marshal of the Rouen expedition will be recalled. It was this urge to direct action which in part caused some of his contemporaries to regard him as rash and impetuous. Actually his judgments were cool and his analyses of combat situations quite careful. These facts were eventually widely recognized. He could hardly have survived a quarter century of almost continuous fighting if he had been reckless. Two other factors helped him gain the reputation for impetuosity. First, Queen Elizabeth, until near the end of his life, thought him so, but this quite evidently was because so often when Essex was involved in awkward situations Williams unfortunately was in his company. Second, there is a tendency to label all Welsh as impetuous, without considering the individual cases.

Williams was also a thoughtful man, and his knowledge of his soldierly trade was impressive. This knowledge was of two kinds. He knew the axioms which a soldier must keep in mind from day to day: never attempt to scale the walls of a town unless one has overwhelming superiority; when besieging a town, expect that the first troops through a breach in the wall will be lost; when being besieged, remember that the fury of the enemy's cannonading is usually spent within twenty-four hours. Besides these commonplaces of day-to-day fighting, Williams was also conscious of the wider aspects of the war. He was a modern soldier in an English army which was behind the times. He saw clearly that the secret of the Spanish army's success was its marvelous discipline. Although in that army, as in any other, some important places were given to inexperienced nobles, still the forces were usually led by men who had spent long years at their trade and had been promoted on merit. He compared the Spanish army in the Netherlands to a university. It was in effect a military academy which was always in session. Williams was also keenly aware of what later military men sometimes forgot to their sorrow: the tremendous

importance of sea power to land operations. He was quite
confident that as long as the English and Dutch controlled
the sea they could maintain themselves in the Netherlands,
and that, conversely, the Spanish could never win. One could,
he pointed out, improve the English-Dutch position in the
Netherlands by striking at Spain in the Indies.

He wrote and thought much about the qualities necessary
for a commander. He realized that the characteristics which
made a good company officer might be different from, even
inadequate for, those of a good commander in chief. He also
thought much about his Dutch employers. He perceived that
their ambiguous and ponderous civil machinery frequently
resulted in military weakness. "True it is," he remarked, "those
that serves many, serves nobody," an almost impossible position
for a commander.

Soldiers, like others under stress, complain a good deal, and
Williams was no exception. The Dutch were a frequent object
of his displeasure. At times he found them ungrateful. They
gave him nothing, not even their good wishes. He endured
many a disgrace at their hands. He longed to quit their service,
but "Hungry dogs must follow such that gives them bread." At
times he felt he would rather be in any place other than Holland.
He might serve under Duke Matthias in Hungary, he might
fight the Turk, or he might fight with the Turks against the
Persians. If he had money he would like to see the wars of
Prester John. At one point, feeling particularly low, he even
thought he might carry a harquebus in Ireland. For a cavalry
officer, a captain of lancers, this was the last desperate alternative. He was persuaded Queen Elizabeth took small account of
him. Getting the Prince of Orange's attention, he felt, was a
hopeless task. So many great personages were importuning the
Prince for money that Williams despaired of ever seeing the
color of his crowns. Williams and his men were frequently
unpaid, an injustice he never endured in silence.

Unbearable as fighting was in cold, wet Holland, Williams took a sneaking enjoyment in it. When an attack was unsuccessful he was fond of saying, "Happy was he that could return first." At the siege of Haarlem, the Spanish employed collapsible towers which supported cages containing riflemen. The Dutch and English became expert at shooting down the towers, and the mortality rate of the riflemen was consequently high. Williams remarked dryly, "So, at last no birds could be found to sing in cages."

Like other soldiers, Williams was apt to alternate hard fighting or strenuous service with equally strenuous diversions. A Welsh officer named Thomas, serving in the Spanish army, once challenged the English commander in the Netherlands, Sir John Norris, to single combat. Norris refused, but Williams took up the challenge. The combat took place within view of the opposing armies. The two valiant Welshmen hacked at each other until it was obvious that neither was quite capable of killing the other, whereupon they called off the duel and went off to have a drinking party together.

One cold December day years later, when the English were besieging Rouen, they had prepared an ambush for the enemy. Sir Roger Williams, Sir Thomas Coningsby, and others lay concealed all morning, but the enemy was wary and did not fall into the trap. About midday, the English gave up the abortive ambush operation. "Sir Roger [Williams] and I," says Coningsby, then "were invited to certain French gentlemen, where we drank carouses; and what, either with the cold of the long expectation in the morning or overmuch wine at dinner, the one side of my head did ache [for] two days after." [52] The event that brought on Williams' death was apparently a bout of overdrinking and overeating, which in turn brought on a fever. It appears possible that, like many another soldier, he had contracted a chronic fever in the Netherlands.

[52] Coningsby, "Journal," pp. 59–60.

Introduction

For most readers, an interesting speculation is whether or not Williams was the archetype for Shakespeare's Fluellen. There can be no doubt that this man of action made a tremendous impression on contemporary writers. The year after Williams' death Thomas Nash characterized him as a noble gentleman, whom "I was excessively beholden to and on whom I have vowed . . . to bestow a memorial epitaph." In Chapman's play *The Conspiracy and Tragedy of Charles, Duke of Byron* (1608), Savoy says to Marshal Byron, putting him in his place, that there was once a Colonel Williams who "made a man that at your most contained you" (III.i). John Davies of Hereford eulogized Williams in his poem *Microcosmos* (1603).

> Now, from the court descend we to the camp,
> And from those elder times to these of ours;
> There find we (no less current for the stamp)
> Williams (world's wonder for his native powers)
> Out-daring Death in many sanguine showers:
> The singing bullets made his soul rejoice
> As music that the hearing most allures,
> And if the cannons bass'd it with their voice,
> He seem'd as ravisht with an heav'nly noise.
>
> · · · · · · · · · · · · ·
>
> And when the foemen's muskets' spite did spit,
> Then would he spit in sport at them the while;
> The blows his courage gave were plac'd by wit,
> For wit and courage dwelt still in his style:
> While cowardice and folly made them vile
> Whose glory lay all in their lady's lap,
> And, when he came to court, at them would smile,
> Yea, smoothly jest at their soft-silken hap,
> Yet could, like Mars, take there sometimes a nap.
>
> · · · · · · · · · · · · ·
>
> Should I recount the petty miracles
> By him performed in his martial course,
> My words would scarce be held for oracles:

Introduction

Sufficeth me the world (that knew his force)
Well knew his heart was Wit and Valor's source,
And they that most envy our British fame
Must needs thus much of him confess (perforce),
That whatsoever from this Briton came
Was wit and sprite, or savor'd of the same.

It is quite possible that Williams also made an impression on Shakespeare, but before one decides that this Welshman is necessarily Shakespeare's Welshman, it is useful to recall that there were many Welsh soldiers prominent at this time. A gallant officer named Thomas fought in the Spanish army, and the Netherlands army lists contain many such names as Morgan, Price, Reed, Owen, Gwynn, and Vaughan. It was in fact a heyday for Welsh soldiers. After all, a countrywoman of theirs was ruling England. The characteristics which Shakespeare gives Fluellen are the stock characteristics ascribed to Welshmen and Welsh soldiers. In some respects Williams was unlike Shakespeare's Welshman. Fluellen was a traditionalist, much attached to the ancient discipline and decorum of combat. He belonged to that most respectable class of people who believe in doing nothing for the first time. Williams, on the contrary, was critical of the past and the present and looked forward to the future. Archers, he felt, were antiquated and inefficient. The English cavalry in his opinion could be improved. The English soldiers first really learned how to handle muskets not in England but on the Continent. If Pelham, he observed, were the great English soldier, then the average was not high. If the illustrious generals of classical times had seen firearms, they would have thrown away their swords, shields, and arrows without a moment's hesitation. Williams' writings are full of such observations. Unlike Fluellen, he was a modern soldier. Fluellen wanted to philosophize about war although the moment called for action. It was the Irish captain, Macmorris, a man after Williams' own heart, who exploded at the idiocy of academic discussion when there was fighting to be done. In battle, Williams' reflexes were the quickest, his analysis the sharpest, his heart the most valiant, his actions the most decisive, of all his comrades. With him fighting came first and philosophizing about war second, or perhaps third—after drinking, merrymaking, and (according to John Davies) wenching.

The book

Williams mentions his intention to write such a volume as the present one in a letter to Walsingham dated from Delft, April 15, 1584. "If the wars fall not hot presently here," he writes, "I will remember all that I saw and learned since the beginning of my time and will cause one to write it. First Your Honor shall have it; if you think good it shall pass further; if not, I trust Your Honor will pardon me for that folly as you have done for many others."[53] Williams thought about the task for six months before he began to write. A letter to Walsingham dated October 27, 1584, from Barnard [*sic*] Castle indicates that he was already well started. "Being idle," he says,

I thought good to write all the actions which passed in the Low Countries since the Duke of Alva's first entry until the Prince's death, where I have busied myself this five days when I had leisure from company. I have passed the siege of Mons, the which put me in some pains by reason I was not at those services; what I do write, it is by good reports, or by experience, being in present with the service.[54]

An interesting point is that between the time when he says he is thinking about writing such a book and the time when he actually began it he had opportunities to talk with the Prince of Orange. It may be that the Prince knew about the proposed book and talked to him at length about the beginnings of the conflict,

[53] *CSP, For., 1583–1584*, p. 458, April 15, 1584.
[54] *CSP, For., 1584–1585*, p. 121, October 27, 1584.

which had occurred before Williams entered his service. Williams' quotations of the Prince's remarks are all from that earlier period.

Since he had already gone beyond the siege of Mons, he must have written one quarter of the present book in those five days in October. One might assume that his enthusiasm and energy did not flag and that he perhaps completed a draft of the present book within the year. But having written a draft, he did nothing with it. Six years later, in 1590, he published an entirely different book, his *Brief Discourse of War*, which is chiefly concerned with three things: first, the duties, techniques, and qualities of military commanders; second, an analysis of the organization and discipline of the Spanish army; and third, a description of the siege of Sluis. Since the siege of Sluis occurred in the summer of 1587, the manuscript, or part of it, can be dated approximately. It was probably written in 1590, when owing to the Queen's displeasure he was forced to be inactive. These remarks have a bearing on the present book, for in his *Brief Discourse of War* he says that he has busied himself "more than two years in writing sundry actions that passed in our days, especially the great actions of the Netherlanders since the first arrival of the Duke of Alva until the last sieges of Sluis and Bruges." In short, the account which was well begun in 1584, he says, was written between 1587 and 1590. Having written the manuscript in English, he goes on to say he intended to publish it in French. Unfortunately, a servant lost part of his papers, so that he had to abandon that ambitious plan and was now publishing part of the original English manuscript. Thus, according to Williams' own statement, his narrative of the Dutch wars and his *Brief Discourse of War* were parts of the same original manuscript.

There is one additional complication. In the present volume Williams refers to his discourse on the Spanish discipline, and the reader must assume that the *Brief Discourse of War*, which describes events in 1587, was written before the present volume, which describes the events of 1568–1573. In 1584 he was well begun on the present manuscript covering the events of 1568– 1573 and may have finished it at that time. By 1590 he is saying that he has worked two years on the narrative and has covered the period 1568–1587. Yet when the present manuscript was published long after his death, it contained words which lead one to suspect that it was written after the *Brief Discourse of War*, which discussed events of 1587.

A book which described events from the Dutch viewpoint, then switched and described succeeding events from the Span- ish view, and then switched a second time and took up the war from the Dutch side, would make an awkward narrative. Yet since Williams wrote from his own experience, that is the way his narrative progressed. The alternative was to write two books; the first an account of events to 1573 from the Dutch viewpoint, and the second (not a narrative) on the Spanish military organization in general, returning at the end of the second volume to a narrative account of the stirring siege of Sluis, probably his most memorable experience.

The present volume was first published in 1618, twenty-three years after Williams' death. It was dedicated by the owner of the manuscript, Sir Peter Manwood, to Sir Francis Bacon. In the dedication Manwood, a patron of learning who was much in- terested in history, says that he has possessed the manuscript a long time. The book was prepared for publication by Sir John Hayward, the historian. He says in his preface that he does not know if the present narrative is complete or if it is only a frag- ment of a longer work. He says that the manuscript came to him "in a ragged hand, much maimed both in sense and in phrase. I have restored it so near as I could both to the style and mean- ing of the author." Only one who has busied himself with Wil- liams' books and letters can fully appreciate that sentence. It ought to be noted that there are two issues of the book, both dated 1618. The differences in the texts of the two editions are negligible except in one instance which occurs on page 15 of both 1618 issues, page 21 of the present edition. Williams' original wording is given in the present edition, which is based on the first issue. Williams' words are:

Being resolved both in Spain and Flanders, he dispatched his great captain and marshal, Chiappino Vitelli, unto Her Majesty with some feigned message; but by all likelihood they had intelligence with our rebels. For immediately after Vitelli's retreat out of England, the Earls of Northumberland and Westmorland were in arms in the North Country, and the Duke of Norfolk discovered himself faulty presently after, at which time the Duke of Alva had ready in Zeeland some ten regiments to embark for England. But by God's providence our rebels were defeated before they could embark.

Apparently Williams' plain speaking was not relished by some, for in the second issue Northumberland and Westmorland were no longer plainly labeled rebels and Norfolk no longer revealed himself as faulty but was merely "charged" with being faulty. The wording of the second issue is:

Being resolved both in Spain and Flanders, he dispatched his great captain and marshal, Chiappino Vitelli, unto Her Majesty with some feigned message; but by all likelihood they had intelligence of our discontents. For immediately after Vitelli's retreat out of England, the Earls of Northumberland and Westmorland were in arms in the North Country, and the Duke of Norfolk was charged as faulty presently after, at which time the Duke of Alva had ready in Zeeland some ten regiments to embark for England. But by God's providence our stirs were quieted before they could embark.

Subsequent to the appearance of the first issues, the text was republished, without editing, in the Somers Tracts, and a Dutch translation of the manuscript was made by a seventeenth-century Dutch general, Jacob Wyts, and published by a Dutch historian, J. T. Bodel Nyenhuis, in the works of the Utrecht

Introduction

Historical Society (new series, no. 3, 1864). In the present edition the spelling and punctuation have been corrected and modernized and notes have been added.

The wars in the Netherlands

The actions which Williams describes here occur during the first battles of the Dutch war against Spain which, with a brief intermission, lasted for eighty years, from 1568 until 1648. At the beginning of the period the Netherlands was part of the dominions of Spain. The war ended with part of the Low Countries, the present Belgium, still under Spain, and the other part, the present Netherlands, independent. The causes of the war were various. The Netherlands in the sixteenth century was one of the richest portions of the Hapsburg dominions; Charles V, the predecessor of Philip II, indulged a prodigious appetite for war and used the wealth of the Netherlands to support this expensive taste. Fifteen years before war broke out in the Netherlands, recrimination between the sovereign and the people, the result of heavy taxation and shortage of money, was already evident.

Added to this difficulty was the fact that the Netherlanders were ruled by an alien people. Charles V was born in the Netherlands and spoke the language of the country, a fact which mitigated the situation; but his son, Philip II, was thoroughly Spanish, ignorant of the Netherlandish language and antipathetic to the country. He found himself at the head of a vast, heterogeneous empire, most of which he had no feeling for. He attempted to make the administration of these domains uniform and rational, both in civil and ecclesiastical matters. In the Netherlands this attempt did violence to many ancient traditions and usages. Thus, in a sense, the resulting war for many Netherlanders was a fight against change and for the continuance of medieval ways. Added to this cause of aggravation was the problem of the nobility. The use of firearms, artillery, and disciplined troop formations had made obsolete the knight in armor wielding his sword against an adversary in single combat. Well-trained, experienced officers who knew army business were much more effective. Civil government had also become complex and likewise required well-trained men. There was little scope for untrained nobility, either in the army or in civil affairs, and they were idle and discontented.

Several years before war broke out, religion also had become an issue. In Spain, heresy was a threat to government. Moslems had been the enemy for centuries. Anyone who deviated from the Christian faith was by that divisive action aiding the enemy. Nowhere in Europe was orthodoxy so highly valued and rigidly maintained. Heterodoxy, on the contrary, had long existed in the Netherlands. This tendency was not troublesome for Spain until the advent of Calvinism, whose adherents frequently refused any compromise with Catholics. Eventually the Calvinists, although a small minority, proved to be the hard core of the opposition to Spain.

As Sir Roger indicates, fighting between Spain and the Prince of Orange and his adherents broke out in 1568. Whenever the two adversaries clashed in the southern part of the country, roughly what is now Belgium, the Netherlanders were usually beaten. Examples of this in Williams' narrative are the siege of Mons and the march of the Prince of Orange through the southern provinces. Whenever the fighting occurred in what is now Holland, the Netherlanders were able to maintain themselves on something like even terms, and here eventually they were successful. Williams' description of the actions at Flushing, Brielle, Middelburg, Goes, and in Groningen are examples of this fact. The two regions, South and North Netherlands, are quite different geographically. The southern region consists of plains and rolling country, ideal for fighting and well deserving its appellation of "the cockpit of Europe." The northern region is cut off from this "cockpit" by great rivers, the Rhine, the Waal, the Ijssel, and the Lek; it is a region of dikes, rivers, lakes, sea-ports, and fortified towns. These geographical facts make Williams' account appear somewhat puzzling. The events he narrates do not sound like war as we know it. They appear to be a series of disconnected actions. Someone has characterized them as a series of desperate scuffles on dikes, of isolated and cruel sieges, of maritime actions in cramped spaces. Actually, because of the geography, that was the nature of war. In the watery regions of the North Netherlands there was no room for maneuvering large bodies of troops.

Another peculiarity of the narrative is that a few battles and marches in 1568 are described; then the narrative jumps to 1572. Seen in modern perspective, the war did lack continuity. When the Netherlanders in 1568 attempted to fight pitched battles in the traditional way they were beaten. When, to some extent by accident, in 1572 they seized and defended towns easily supplied by water, the war revived and was successful. The decisive factor, as Williams plainly saw, was sea power. Although his details are sometimes faulty, the present book gives an accurate impression of war as it was actually fought in the Netherlands at the time. Williams' account has interested both the Dutch and English for 450 years. It is hoped that the present edition will extend this interest.

THE ACTIONS OF
THE LOW COUNTRIES

By Sir Roger Williams

To the Right Honorable Sir Francis Bacon, Knight, Lord Chancellor of England

RIGHT HONORABLE:

This part of history, having lain a long time by me, I have thought good to publish to the world, and that especially for these reasons: first, to incite other men of arms to imitate in like sort their great master Julius Caesar, who wrote exact commentaries (adorned of late with observations of a worthy man of our nation) of such military actions as happened under his command; secondly, to prevent lest such worthy pains should either perish or hereafter be set forth by others as their own, a thing too much practiced by some, not of meanest note; lastly, to make this a mean of drawing the residue into light, which haply sleepeth in the custody of some other man. This do I presume to present to your Honor, as well in regard of the honorable estimation which still remaineth of the author, as for the worthiness which I conceive to be in the work. For all of us do well discern both the luster of many excellent perfections in your own noble spirit and how you favor men of valor, learning, or honest endeavor: which virtues, as they have advanced you to this height of honor, so will they make your memory eternally to flourish.

Your Honor's in all service,
PE[TER] MANWOOD

St. Stephens
1 January, 1617

To the Reader

ALBEIT in all histories three things are especially required, order, poise, and truth, yet for divers causes it happeneth that in many one of these doth fail.

For some have written of times so anciently past that no means are extant either to direct or to correct them. Many of these, living in artless ages, have stuffed their stories with most senseless fictions, nothing better than countrywomen's tales. Of this sort was Hunibaldus, who fableth that the French took their original from Francio, a Trojan, and is followed in his sotteries by Gregory of Tours, Rheginus, Sigebert, and divers others of the same suite.[1] After this example, Geoffrey of Monmouth about four hundred years since did first (as some affirm) draw the original of the Britons from Brutus, the Trojan, forging such races, names, reigns, and passages of affairs as may more easily be convinced to be false than supplied with any certain truth. Of the same strain is Wittikind, who by his counterfeit Saxo hath drawn the Saxons and first inhabitants of Germany from the old Macedonian soldiers of Alexander the Great. So the Scots set up Scota, daughter to Pharaoh, King of Egypt, for foundress of their nation. Likewise the Irish hatched their Hiberus, the Danes their Danus, the Brabants their Brabo, the Goths their Gothus, as founders both of their nation and name, a subject wherein forgeries may range at large, because the

---

[1] Where it is possible to establish authoritative modern spellings for proper names, such spellings have been adopted. In all other cases we have left the proper names as spelled by the author.

first times of nations for the most part are, as very small, so altogether obscure. Of this sort among the ancients were Herodotus, Diodorus Siculus, and Theopompus, in whose books, Cicero saith, many idle untruths are found, even so far as the vain vein of the Grecians durst adventure to advow for truths. In how many places (saith Josephus) is Hellanicus charged with falsities by Agesilaus and by Ephorus, they by Timaeus, Timaeus by many who followed, Herodotus by all?

Others have written of countries far distant, either altogether unknown or by them never seen, who, writing upon vulgar reports things either imagined or erroneously observed, are easily entangled with untruths. Of this fault Eratosthenes, Poseidonius, and Patrocles the geographer are branded by Strabo. Hence also did rise the fables of the Arimasps, gryphons, Troglodytes, Amazons, satyrs, Pygmies, and of their cruel wars with cranes; of nations of men with dogs' heads, with horse feet, without heads, without mouths, with one foot wherewith they cover themselves against sun and rain, and of divers other monstrous kinds of men, beasts, and fowls, which now are discovered for Utopical aperies. With these may Stephanus and Arrianus be joined, of whom the one writeth that the French are a people of Italy, the other placeth the Germans near to the Ionic Sea. So Strabo choppeth that the river Ister or Danowe [Danube] hath his spring near to the Adriatic Sea and that the rivers Lapus [Lippe?] and Vezer [Weser] discharge themselves into the river Enis [Ems], whereas the one runneth into the Rhine, the other into the ocean. So are Tacitus, Marcellus, Orosius, Blondus [Flavio Biondo] in divers places of Germany much mistaken. And so Sabellicus, Volaterrane, and Conrade do much confound the Alans and Almans, the Hungarians and Huns, the Danes and the Dacc, Austerane and Austrich, placing the Mount Saint Ottoly in Bavaria and the Riphaean Mountains in Polonia or Muscovia.

Others have written of their own countries and times, but these again are of divers sorts. For some busy themselves much in those things which the popular multitude do applaud, making wordy (I cannot say worthy) reports of bearbaitings, launching of ships, fleas, mice, owls, masques, mayings, etc. And if they speak of any public affairs they discern nothing but the outside, not unlike to beggars who traverse over many countries from door to door and touch as many fair buildings but observe nothing either of the persons or furniture or order within. Such historians do daily and duly attend certain kings in India, and whatsoever they do, whether eat, drink, sleep, disport, ease nature, retire to any woman, in a word, *all*, they barely write down, and nothing else.

Some others, better furnished with judgment, do strongly bias in their affections and that chiefly by two means, levity and partiality. Of the first sort are they who, affecting to write rather pleasingly than truly, do interlace many jests, conceits, tales, and other pleasing passages, either omitting or defacing the solid truth. Of this fault Trebellius is reproved by Laberian and Vopiscus, Tacitus by Tertullian and Orosius, Orosius by Blondus. To these also we may adjoin Danudes, Philostratus, Guidius, Cresias, Hecataeus, and divers others who have transformed the truth of many things into fabulous inventions of their own. Of the second sort are they who upon hate, fear, or favor, either to some persons, or to their native country, or to the religion which they profess, or for some other partial respect, do write panegyrics or invectives rather than histories. So Sallust writeth that the acts of the Grecians are much admired, not because they exceed the achievements of other men, but because their writers, having wit at will, did much enlarge them above the truth. Of this fault Blondus and Sabellicus are noted in their histories of Venice, Paulus Aemilius and Gaguin in their histories of France, and most others in the histories of their own countries, who extol, depress, deprave immoderately, making things seem not as they are but as they would have them, no otherwise almost than comedies and tragedies are fashioned by their authors.

The Actions of the Low Countries

Amongst those few who have written with knowledge, judgment, and sincerity, the author of this history is worthy to be ranged, who doubtless was of endless industry, always in action, either with his sword or with his pen. He was well known to be a man who both knew and durst, his courage no less free from indiscretion than from fear. Yet hath he wrote so modestly of himself that some may haply esteem him rather a looker-on than a meddler in the hot medleys whereof he doth write; but his attributing so little to himself will make others attribute the more unto him. In writing of others he expresseth a most generous disposition, neither forbearing the errors of his friends nor forgetting the vigilancy and valor of his enemies, but carrying himself with an even hand between them.

Touching the history itself, it is faithful and free, wherein are found sieges, assaults, surprises, ambushes, skirmishes, battles, lively described; great variety both of persons and of actions; much mutability of fortune, many changes in affairs; admirable advices, unexpected events, ponderous judgments; a phrase in a soldier's style, sinewy and sweet, full both of perspicuity and grace. In a word, I esteem it a complete history, if it were complete. I mean, if it extended to all the actions wherein the author did serve. But whether the residue was never written, or whether it be perished, or whether it resteth in any other hand, I remain doubtful. This piece, being showed to me by a person of whose virtues I had rather speak nothing than not enough, I did much esteem, for that it compriseth some actions of the time wherein I have lived; of which time I endeavor to leave a large memorial to posterity. But, coming to me in a ragged hand, much maimed both in sense and in phrase, I have restored it so near as I could both to the style and meaning of the author. This is all the pains that I have taken. This is all the thanks which I do either challenge or deserve.

Jo[HN] HAYWARD

The occasions of the first stirs in the Low Countries; the Duke of Alva's first coming thither, and his surprising of the principal of the nobility; the Prince of Orange escapeth into Germany, and Charles Mansfeld into France

THE state of Spain, as I said in my discourse of their discipline, is governed by two sorts of people, captains and clergy. The captains animate the King to wars to maintain their wealth and greatness; so doth the clergy to maintain their estate against them of the religion.[1] By these means, the ambition of the Duke of Alva, of Cardinal Granvelle, and their seconds, persuaded the King to undertake to subdue the Netherlanders to his pleasure, to lay upon them such gables,[2] taxes, and all manner of tributes as should please the King to demand. But this they could never effect without making away their warlike and politic nobility; namely, the Prince of Orange, the Counts of Egmond, of Hoorne, of Batenburg, the Lord of Brederode, the Marquis of Bergen, with divers others of good quality. Besides they had a great number of strong towns, innumerable treasure and riches, the seat of the most of their provinces being marvelous strong by nature, by reason of their great rivers and straits, furnished plentifully with artillery, munition, and other necessaries for wars. Also their liberties were such that no stranger might govern either their provinces or any of their towns. And this grieved

[1] Against the Calvinists. Williams sometimes uses the phrase to denote both the Calvinists and Lutherans.

[2] Taxes, or excise duties; cf. French *gabelle,* originally a salt tax.

9

the Spanish not a little, that such base people as they esteemed the Netherlanders to be should possess peaceably such a brave and rich country and their King carry no other title than Duke, Count, and Lord over their seventeen provinces. Hereupon the King resolved to send his great captain, the Duke of Alva, with a mighty army, giving him commission to alter, place, and displace whom and as many as pleased him, as well in their provinces in general as in any particular town, also giving him authority to execute as many as pleased him without respect of persons.

This being discovered unto the Prince of Orange from a gentleman Burgundian of the King's chamber (who was greater with one of the King's secretaries' wives than with her husband), by reason of the Spanish long counsels in their resolutions, it came in good time to the Prince, long before the Duke's troops marched from Spain into Italy. In the meantime the Prince animated the people all he could against the Spanish, making divers of his assured friends acquainted with his intelligences, but durst not trust Count Egmond, fearing his ambition and choler would mar all. Notwithstanding, considering his vogue and greatness with the men of war, he durst attempt nothing without him. Wherefore, politicly, the Prince fed both parties, assured the Governess, the Duchess of Parma, of his loyalty toward the King and his religion; but in troth he was of the Protestant religion, favoring them what he could underhand, so much, that he and his instruments procured the people in great numbers to present supplications openly to the Governess for the liberty of their consciences. Likewise divers papists and Martinists [3] presented her with supplications to persuade the King to stay his Duke of Alva and his armies, showing her plainly that it was against their liberty and customs that strangers should govern them.

In this time the Prince and his instruments animated a quar-

[3] Lutherans.

rel betwixt Count Egmond and Cardinal Granvelle, so as
after a banquet at Brussels, upon a dispute with multiplying of
words, the Count took the Cardinal a box on the ear, to the
Prince and his party's great joy.[4] This Count (as I said before)
was so ambitious that he thought it his due to be chief over all
warlike actions which either King or his country would undertake (I mean among the Netherlanders); without comparison
he deserved it. He was most valiant, most liberal, and greatly
fortunate in all his actions. Amongst the rest of his actions, the
chief praise of the Battle of Saint-Quentin and of Gravelines belonged to this Count. Notwithstanding, the Prince of Orange
carried all the vogue amongst the popular by his fine and politic government and won a number of men of quality with great
courtesies and affable discourses, insomuch that these two
chiefs, being joined, would have carried all the country in general to have done what they had listed.

After this disgrace, the Cardinal very politicly showed neither choler nor mind to revenge, but rather sought all means
underhand to stay the Count from proceeding further with the
Prince; and both he and the Governess procured letters from the
King with great speed to that end, in which letters were contained that nothing should be done in the Netherlands, as well
by the Duke of Alva as by his base sister the Governess, without the Count's consent, and to repose all trust in the Count
only for martial affairs. The King wrote also unto the Count assuring him that nothing should be too dear for him and that his
great service should not be forgotten but recompensed to the
highest degree, showing him how all these stirs proceeded from
the Prince of Orange and his instruments, to overthrow religion
and to maintain his estate and greatness. Besides, they sent
counterfeit letters unto the Count as though the Prince or his faction had certified the King often against the Count to his dis-

---

[4] The story that Egmond boxed Cardinal Granvelle's ear cannot be sub-
stantiated.

grace. Before these posts arrived, the Prince or his instruments had procured the Count and all or most of the nobility, with a great number of quality, to meet at Tilmount [5] in Brabant, where, after a great banquet, most of them signed a letter to the King rather to die than to suffer the government to alter. This letter was written very humbly to persuade His Majesty to stay his Duke of Alva, assuring him to be loyal in all points, desiring His Majesty to remember their liberties and customs, which His Majesty was sworn to maintain in as ample a manner as his ancestors before. At this banquet all signed these letters, saving the Count Pieter Ernst of Mansfeld, Governor of Luxembourg, and the Lord of Berlaymont, who politicly promised to do the like the next morning, excusing themselves that at that instant the wine was their master. But at midnight they stole post toward Luxembourg, excusing themselves by letters unto the Prince of Orange that Count Egmond would be debauched from them by the Spanish instruments and that they would not believe the contrary until they heard that his person and men of war were in battle against the Spanish. It seems Pieter Ernst was willing to second them, for he left his son, Count Charles, as deep as the best.

They had reason to fear the Count [Egmond], for the next day he began to repent him of his bargain, taking occasions to murmur and to stir factions against the Prince. But the Prince politicly courtesied him with all favors, in such sort that all fell in a banquet the next dinner, at which feast, according to their custom, there was great carousing, where the basest sort came in great multitudes with glasses in their hands, crying to the Prince, Count, and nobility, *Vive les gueux, vive les gueux, le diable emporte les Espagnoles* (God save the beggars, and the

[5] Bodel Nyenhuis (see Introduction, p. xlvi) suggests Turnhout. It is also possible Williams meant Tilburg. The conversation which Williams reports between Orange and Egmond is one which is said to have taken place at Willebroek in April, 1567.

devil take the Spaniards). After ending the banquet, the Prince procured many of the nobility and of the best sort to promise to second him in the action he would undertake against the Spanish. This being discovered unto Count Egmond, he commanded his horses and coaches to be made ready, seeming to be much offended with the Prince of Orange and his faction, and withal departed toward Louvain.

True it is, all murders are villainous, but had the Prince credited Count Charles Mansfeld, Count Egmond had been dead. I heard the Prince relate his counsel, which was: "Let us kill Count Egmond; then are we sure all the men of war will follow you and yours. Also his countenance is such amongst them as at his reconcilement unto the Spanish they will all follow him. But for fear of him, my father and all the rest would join with you." True it is, this young gentleman [Count Charles] was the willfulest amongst them but spake the greatest reason to maintain the Prince of Orange, as it fell out afterwards, for without doubt the reconcilement of Count Egmond lost himself and all his friends. Long afterwards in France I heard Count Charles speak this, and also how he would have wished the Prince afterwards to have marched with all his forces unto the edge of Lorraine, there to have kept the straits betwixt Lorraine and Luxembourg, where the Duke of Alva must pass without all doubt. With the favor of God, had the Prince and Count Egmond marched thither with their forces, by all reason they might have fought with twice the Duke of Alva's numbers; for there were four thousand brave lancers and light horsemen under their charge, ready, always entertained, besides as many more who would have mounted themselves most willingly with at least twenty thousand footmen against the Spanish and [with] the Prince had they made away the obstinate Count. Besides, the nature of the Netherlanders is to be very willing to second any novelties, much more against a people they hated so much as the Spanish, whose forces and policies were unknown to them at their beginning. Being as high as Lorraine, they had been sure all the countries and towns behind them would have seconded them with all necessaries; for the humor of the nation is to be unreasonable proud with the least victory or advancement with a reasonable army and deadly fearful with the least overthrow or at the retreat of their men of war from their enemy.

The posts being arrived with the Governess and Cardinal (who received express commandment from the King to dissemble his disgrace with the Count, assuring him the Duke of Alva should redress all), Count Egmond, having received the King's letters, fell clean from the Prince unto the Governess and began to make all the fair weather he could unto the Cardinal, thinking himself sure. This poor Count persuaded all the rest to forsake their Prince, assuring them that he would undertake to make all well again with the King, in such sort that most of the nobility quitted the Prince, who, fearing that the variable popular would do the like, resolved to acquaint Count Egmond what the King had passed against them in his Spanish council; and, opening his mind unto divers of the best sort, the Prince procured Count Egmond, with most of the rest, to give him audience, whose words I heard the Prince himself report as followeth:

Cousins and dear countrymen, it grieves me to see you so blinded with the Spanish dissimulation, which is to no other end but to lull you asleep until their tyrant D'Alva arrives amongst us, who hath so large a commission. And this he will not fail to execute to the uttermost, which he can never do and suffer us to live, especially you, Count Egmond. And resolve yourself that they who send him with such directions know your courage to be too great to endure your countrymen to be made slaves and to suffer him to wash his hands in your kinsmen's blood. Believe my words, it is true what I tell you; for there you see his hand, whom divers of you know to be in good credit with the King, especially with his principal secretary.

And herewith he cast his letter with other testimonials amongst them, telling the Count, "Cousin, resolve on it, if you take arms, I will join with you; if not, I must leave you and quit the country."

After pausing awhile, the Count answered,

Cousin, I know the King hath not Spaniards enow to employ in all his dominions, wherefore you must think he must be served by others more than Spaniards. You are deceived to judge the King a tyrant without proof of cruelty; he cannot be so ungrateful to recompense our services with such payments. Touching the Duke of Alva, if it be the King's pleasure to make him Governor of these countries, we must obey him as we did the Duke of Savoy and others. Touching our government, resolve yourself, he will not neither shall alter it more than the rest of his predecessors before him have done. For yourself, if it please you to stay, I dare adventure my credit to make all well with the King, and assure you, doth the Duke of Alva lay hands on you, I will not endure it.

Withal he hurled before the Prince and the rest the King's letters, wherein was no want of dissimulation nor of promise of forgiveness, only to be assured to bring them sound asleep until the Duke of Alva should awake them. Herewith the Count told the Prince resolutely that he would not quit the King. If he would not stay, it would grieve him to see his house overthrown.

The Prince answered,

Cousin, I have been too long by his father's chamber, and do know the King's humors too well and their Spanish government, to conceive that they will pardon such persons as a number of us here be, after entering into such actions as we have done against them. Good cousin, do you forget how the Duke of Alva was wont to say unto Charles the Fifth: *Hombres muertos no hazen guerra:* "Dead men make no war." For these reasons and divers others, farewell. I will not stay their justice nor trust to their courtesies. For house it makes no matter; I had rather be a prince without houses than a count without a head.

The Actions of the Low Countries

During these treaties and delays, divers brawls and bickerings fell out in Antwerp betwixt them of the religion,[6] the Martinists, and papists. Twice or thrice a week great numbers would be in arms, sometimes before the Governess' court, sometimes before the Prince of Orange's house, but often or continually in places of greatest note. Although the Prince was most politic, yet his courage was nothing comparable to a number of others; if it had, without doubt he might have hazarded to have surprised Antwerp. Having done it, he might have engaged the rest of the country; for in Ghent and in the great towns was faction for religion, especially throughout the most of the villages and countries, where was preaching and defacing of images in many places, insomuch that the papists and Martinists drew them of the religion out of Antwerp. Notwithstanding, they gathered together at a village hard by Antwerp called Austruweel, where they preached in great numbers in such sort that the Governess and all hers stood in doubt whether it were best to hazard their defeat there or to stay for more forces.

Being considered how they increased daily, resolution was taken to charge them where they were, intelligence being brought them that the papists and Martinists with a number of soldiers did sally to defeat them. Notwithstanding they were void of any men of conduct or soldiers gaged under ensigns or cornets,[7] and all, or the most, craftsmen, mechanics, or poor peasants, yet they resolved to fight, making head with good courage against their enemies. But for want of heads to direct them, default of arms and munition, they were defeated in plain field. Judge you what they would have done being in the town of Antwerp, having with them a Prince of Orange, who

[6] Calvinists.

[7] Here Williams uses the words "ensigns and cornets" to mean infantry and cavalry officers. Elsewhere he uses the words to mean the flags or standards carried by companies of infantry and troops of cavalry. In still other places he means the companies and troops themselves. The words were long used in all three senses.

had with him continually two or three hundred gentlemen, divers of charge and conduct. Besides he was Governor of the town, never without a good party, so as the Governess and hers durst not lay hands on him although they knew him an enemy and a favorer of the religion. To say truth, he cloaked it what he could, insomuch as, all their parties being often in arms in the great places, himself went to the strongest, which were the papists and Martinists, protesting to them to live and die with the Governess and religion. Without doubt his meaning was, touching the Governess, to be true to his country and to live and die with the religion. For amongst them of the religion he had divers instruments, some of his best gentlemen and captains, who (God knows) at that time had but little skill in wars, notwithstanding they were assured by them of his good will, in such sort that they would have marched often against the others but for the Prince's persuasions to the contrary. Sometimes he would tell them their enemies were more in number, and in charging them they should engage their town, wives, children, and goods, assuring them if they would go forward the basest sort would ransack their houses. Since, I heard the Prince say that if he had known the wars then so well as he did since he would have ranged on their sides, wishing then his valiant brother Count Ludwig in his place. Pity or fear overthrew the Prince often, as I will show hereafter. Great warriors account the pitiful captain a fool in wars and never cruel until he masters his enemy; then he must be bloody to execute, if he cannot live in safety.

This order continued until the news came that the Duke of Alva was marching. Then it was high time for the Prince to shift for himself. Before he [8] arrived, the Prince was in Germany. After, moving the whole state of the Empire except the house of Austria, he found little comfort at their hands, saving the Count Palatine of the Rhine and his own house of Nassau, not without marvel, for those phlegmatic people will second nobody

[8] The Duke of Alva.

without money beforehand and assurance to be paid monthly, especially being gaged to serve the weakest party. When they come into the field, they will endure neither hardness nor wants without their due *geld*.[9] When they have joined battle, they have often cried *"Geld,"* hurled their weapons from them, and suffered their enemies to cut them in pieces. I do persuade myself all potentates and estates hire them, only fearing their enemies would have them. Without doubt, if one side hath them and not the other, likely it is master of the field. They come in such multitudes of horsemen as no Christian nation besides is able to furnish. Else, persuade yourself, 500 of either English, Scottish, Burgundians, Walloons, French, Italians, Albanese, Hungarians, Poles, or Spanish is worth 1,500 Almains.

The Duke of Alva being arrived in Lorraine, Count Pieter Ernst [van Mansfeld], Governor of Luxembourg, feared him, but like a wise politic man sent unto him to offer him all service. Notwithstanding, he kept himself in his strong towns of Luxembourg and Thionville, having garrisons at his devotion, the governors and captains either his kinsmen or assured friends. Neither would he suffer the Duke of Alva to enter those towns or any other under his government of any strength, except only his own person, with so many more as the governors could dispose of at their pleasures. The Duke of Alva, knowing this man to be a very expert valiant captain, would not offend him, but rather pleased him all that he might. Insomuch as he procured divers favorable letters from the King, to encourage him of their good meaning toward him, fearing otherwise that it lay in him to give the Duchy of Luxembourg to whom he listed, which might have been a good present to the French king, being joined with Metz in Lorraine.

The Duke of Alva remained quiet in the King's state at Brussels, with some tyrannous Spaniards about him, who from the highest to the lowest gaped for the spoils and confusion of the

[9] German for money.

poor Netherlanders. These (God knows) at that instant were better fed than taught in martial discipline (except a few of their nobility and men of war, who were all at the devotion of the Duke of Alva, by means of the ignorance and obstinacy of Count Egmond, who was deceived and lulled asleep in his vainglory by certain treacherous, tyrannous, and ungrateful Spaniards), insomuch as they refused neither the tenth penny [10] nor any other demands that pleased the Duke of Alva to charge upon them.

The Duke of Alva, having entrapped the Counts of Egmond and Hoorne with divers others of great quality, sent for them to counsel. At their entry into a chamber where he was, the great Provost arrested them of high treason, taking from them their rapiers and arms. You may easily judge their sentences when they were to be tried by the Cardinal Granvelle and his friends. So, for the box on the ear and other follies, Count Egmond lost his head, with divers others, and principally the men of best quality whom they feared and mistrusted to have any vogue with the popular or means to annoy them either with forces or counsel. At this instant Count Charles Mansfeld had with him a vigilant politic companion which his father (the old fox) had foisted into the service of the Duke of Alva only to advertise him and his son of their proceedings. This espial [11] ran to Charles into a tennis court and brought him presently into his lodging, where they mounted themselves speedily to recover Luxembourg; which they did, although the Duke of Alva sent divers others on the spur to bring them to him dead or alive. These missed them narrowly, for they had not passed the bridge of Namur but the others were in the place within one hour.

Returning to the Duke of Alva, he was in great choler for not entrapping Count Charles, and not without reason, for, having him, he might have held him prisoner for the better assurance

[10] A sales tax of 10 per cent levied upon all articles sold.
[11] A spy. Williams spells the word "espy-all."

of his father. The Duke of Alva dispatched present posts to the great Provost of Ardennes, who was altogether at his devotion, by reason of a pick [12] betwixt Count Mansfeld and him. By good espial [13] Count Mansfeld was advertised of their practice, which was that the Provost should use all diligence and means to entrap the father or the son. If both, he should do the King and him great service. Count Charles, being advertised of the match, used all means possible to meet the Provost at equal hands. This Count was rather desperate than valiant in all his quarrels, but politic and full of wit in all his affairs. By good espials [14] he met this Provost, having with him about twenty horsemen, all or the most his own servants. The Count had about twelve, the most or all captains and soldiers. This encounter (God knows) was far against the Provost's will, considering the match, for most men of judgment in those affairs value six chosen men well mounted worth twenty *ramassées,*[15] as the French term them. The Count (as of greatest courage) began to speak as followeth:

Master Provost, I do understand the Duke of Alva commands you to bring my father or myself unto him and that you gave your word you would do it. All honest men ought to maintain their words and promises, especially great officers of quality like yourself. I must confess you ought to obey the King's lieutenant, but not to make promise of more than you are able to perform. You know my father, myself, and you are neighbors' children and kinsmen afar off. Wherefore, for all your small pick, you might have used the Duke with less assurance. But to give him and all his proud Spaniards to understand that a Netherlander carrieth as good resolution as any Spaniard, and to terrify such base fellows as thou art from the like attempt, there is for thee.

And withal struck him with a pistol in his bosom down from his horse. Himself and his company, mastering the rest, ex-

---

[12] Quarrel.

[13] The word is here used in the other sense, the action of spying.

[14] See above.　　　[15] Men scraped together; noncombatants and servants.

ecuted no more, all yielding to his mercy. The Count told them,

Upon condition that some of you will tell the Duke of Alva that I wished him here with his Provost, I give you all your lives and leave to go where you list. Tell him also I am gone to the French king, and from him to the Turk, rather than to yield to his mercy.

The Count, being in France, was greatly favored and well used by the French king and remained there until Don John of Austria came into the Low Countries to be Governor and Captain General. As I said before, Count Pieter Ernst would never hazard himself at the mercy of the Duke of Alva, notwithstanding there passed courteous letters of dissimulation betwixt them. The Duke of Alva all this while played *gloria patri*, as pleased him, thinking his work at an end in the Low Countries saving the finishing of two citadels, the one at Antwerp and the other at Flushing. In the meantime, he, the Cardinal, and others persuaded the King all they might to undertake the conquest of England, thinking thereby to oppress religion in all other places. Being resolved both in Spain and Flanders, he dispatched his great captain and marshal, Chiappino Vitelli, unto Her Majesty with some feigned message; but by all likelihood they had intelligence with our rebels. For immediately after Vitelli's retreat out of England, the Earls of Northumberland and Westmorland were in arms in the North Country, and the Duke of Norfolk discovered himself faulty presently after, at which time the Duke of Alva had ready in Zeeland some ten regiments to embark for England. But by God's providence our rebels were defeated before they could embark. Also God blinded his affairs in such sort that he undertook to finish the citadel of Antwerp before that of Flushing, to his undoing, as I will show in this discourse.

Count Ludwig's entry into Friesland, and the defeat of the Count of Arenberg

I can speak little touching the first journey Count Ludwig made to Friesland; but I heard the Prince report that Count Ludwig marched into Friesland with some 2,500 horsemen and 7,000 footmen, all Germans. And having intelligence with the Count of Schouwenburg and his brother-in-law, the Count van den Bergh, he took the castle of Wedle, with divers other places in Friesland, having engaged Groningen. The Counts of Arenberg and Meghen were dispatched from the Duke of Alva to stop his courses, having with them the master of the camp, Don Gonzalo de Bracamonte, with his Tercio of Sardinia [16] and some companies of Walloons, Geldrois, and Almans,[17] with the two bands of ordnance [18] of the Counts, and about five other cornets,[19] lancers, and argoletiers, Albanese and Walloons. Count Arenberg carried the commission and marched before with Bracamonte and other bands of footmen, giving charge to Count Meghen to follow him speedily with the rest. Count Arenberg, being arrived within two leagues of Count Ludwig and understanding his forces, would have stayed from Count Meghen,[20] who would have been with him that night. The pride of Bracamonte and divers of his Spaniards was such as, valuing Ludwig and his forces as nothing, they urged Count Arenberg with heinous words; insomuch that a number of the basest sort of Spaniards began to call him cowardly traitor, although Count

[16] A tercio was a troop formation, consisting of 10 or 12 companies, 5 of pikes and 5 of harquebusiers, or 6 of pikes and 6 of harquebusiers, together with a regimental band, chaplains, and medical corps. When the Tercio of Sardinia first entered the Netherlands, it consisted of 1,800 men.
[17] Germans.   [18] A company of mounted men in armor.
[19] I.e., about five other squadrons of cavalry, lancers, and argoletiers. An argoletier was a light horseman armed with a musket or harquebus.
[20] "For Count Meghen" makes better sense.

Arenberg was a valiant expert captain and only would have stayed for more forces. For he knew, and all the world with him, that Ludwig was a most valiant, obstinate executioner, who always directed his troops to fight in good order and so resolutely that at an encounter with the French he and Count Mansfeld made a discreet valiant retreat. The Admiral [21] and his Frenchmen being defeated, Bracamonte and his Spaniards urged the Count to approach Ludwig, who was lodged in a village by Groningen, having on both sides broad highways both toward Groningen and his enemies. At the end of the lane toward the enemy there was a great heath with three highways entering unto it. True it is, Ludwig's companions were Germans, but of the best sort; for five hundred of his horsemen were gentlemen that accompanied him and his brother Count Adolf of Nassau for good will. All his rest were a thousand horsemen which he led himself.

Count Arenberg, being approached Count Ludwig's quarters, divided his horsemen on both sides of his footmen, which marched in one squadron conducted by Bracamonte. He placed some five hundred shot [22] before his squadron, the rest on both his sides. Count Arenberg himself led the right wing of the horsemen, his lieutenant of Friesland the left wing. He commanded the argoletiers to march before the forlorn shot of his battle [23] on foot and with some fifty argoletiers to keep as nigh Ludwig's quarters as they could and to keep sentinel at the entry of the lane into the plain. Count Ludwig's couriers [24] having discovered them at the Nuse, Ludwig advanced out of the village, commanding two hundred reiters [25] to displace Arenberg's couriers and to stand in the mouth of the strait. Ludwig came with all his forces, placed his lieutenant, Hendrik van

[21] Admiral Coligny. [22] Musketeers.
[23] I.e., musketeers acting as skirmishers or scouts in advance of the main body of troops.
[24] Scouts or skirmishers.
[25] German cavalry armed with pistols—pistoleers.

Siegen, with a squadron of pikes, some thirty score [26] in the plain; half of his shot on both sides of his squadron; advanced the two hundred reiters thirty score before his battle; [27] placed his brother Count Adolf with six hundred reiters on the right wing of his battle, and so many more with one of his best captains on the left wing. The rest he hid in two squadrons in both the out-lanes, leaving in the middle lane a good squadron of pikes, with some three hundred shot in the hedges on both sides. He gave charge to the two hundred reiters to skirmish with all courage; gave directions to his brother to retire softly as the enemy approached, himself standing with some seven hundred of the best horsemen, hidden in the right lane from the enemy; and gave order to the other wing to run through the pikes which stood in the middlemost lane, who had directions to shift themselves over the hedge as though they were defeated.

His directions were no sooner given but Arenberg's couriers and his were together by the ears and the Nassauians forced to retire under their battles [28] of pikes. Arenberg advanced with all speed both horse and foot. Being near, Bracamonte and his Spanish cried to Count Arenberg to charge; withal, Arenberg and his lieutenant charged at once. According to direction, Count Adolf retired, bringing Count Arenberg (who had by far the greatest wing) on Count Ludwig. So did the other bring Arenberg's lieutenant through the lane where the pikes were. Ludwig, giving sign to his reiters in the third lane to charge, withal chargeth himself and found Count Arenberg and his lieutenant good cheap, [29] by reason they were out of order in running after Adolf's troops. His lieutenant, Hendrik van Siegen, was broken by the Spanish and Walloons; but at the sight of their horsemen, which were in rout, their courage quailed, in such sort that valiant Ludwig ran through them cheap. In

[26] Thirtyscore paces.   [27] His main body of troops.
[28] That is, under their formations of pikes.
[29] Easily defeated or disposed of.

this place the Count of Arenberg was slain, all or most of the Tercio de Sardinia slain or taken prisoners with a number of Walloons and Geldrois. Divers Spanish captains escaped by recovering their horses, which were led not far from them. So did divers Walloons and many of their horsemen, by reason Ludwig executed the most of his fury on the Spanish footmen. At the return of the Spanish captains that escaped, the Duke of Alva executed them, as I showed in my discourse of their discipline, for urging their general to their overthrow.

๙

Count Ludwig essays Groningen, and the Duke of Alva overthrows him at Dam in Friesland

After this, Count Ludwig ransacked Friesland at his pleasure, insomuch that he besieged the fair and rich town of Groningen. The Duke of Alva, hearing this, dispatched his marshal, otherwise called master of the camp, General Chiappino Vitelli, with sufficient troops of horsemen and footmen, being joined with Count de Meghen, to stop Ludwig's course. The Duke of Alva used all diligence to gather his whole forces, who marched with all speed after Vitelli. Vitelli being arrived by Groningen, Ludwig retired his siege into one quarter, resolving to give Vitelli battle, to which end he sent his trumpets [30] to Vitelli to dare him, a small river being betwixt both. Vitelli kept the passages, brake the bridges, answered Count Ludwig he had no order to give battle but to discharge [31] the town of Groningen, delaying the Count politicly and telling his messengers, "I will send unto my general to obtain his good will. Your master may be assured, having leave, a battle will be my first business."

The Duke of Alva being arrived with his fair army within a

[30] Trumpeters were used as heralds or messengers.
[31] Break the siege of Groningen.

day's journey of Vitelli, Count Ludwig retired into Jemmingen, a village by Nye Zyhle [32] toward Emden, breaking the bridges after him. At the end of the village toward the enemy he left Hendrik van Siegen, his lieutenant, with all his infantry, being some eight thousand, which were increased by reason of his good success at the last battle. This Jemmingen was a place environed with waters, saving two or three large ways which came into it from Groningen. On every way Count Ludwig made trenches, placed strong guards, ranged his horsemen in four squadrons, making what means he could to fill ditches, to enlarge grounds, to make ways for his horse to fight out of the highways in divers of the meadows toward Nye Zyhle. By reason of the straits, his horsemen stood behind the footmen in the great ways. Hendrik van Siegen, having entrenched himself reasonably strong with five thousand men to defend the place against the enemy, planted divers fieldpieces which flanked the quarter where the enemy must attempt. Hearing the Duke of Alva's couriers advanced within the sight of the Nassauians' guards, Ludwig sent two hundred reiters to re-encounter them, giving them charge to stop their course what they could, to win time to strengthen his trenches, which were in working with all his hands. Being re-encountered, both these couriers fell into a hot skirmish. Julián Romero, having the vanguard with Robles, seconded their couriers with some four or five hundred argoletiers, in such sort that the Nassauians were forced to retire on the spur. At the sight whereof Ludwig passed some four hundred reiters commanded by a valiant man, who charged the Spaniards into the squadrons which Julián [Romero] and the other led, being four regiments of Spaniards and Walloons. The Grand Prior, the Duke of Alva's son, commanded the battle, having with him Don Juan de Mendoza, general of the horsemen with Vitelli. They passed with all speed through the vanguard some seven hundred lanc-

[32] The account by the Spanish general Verdugo makes it certain that Nye Zyhle is meant.

ers, which chased the Nassauians into their infantry. And withal Julián [Romero] and Robles advanced with all speed. So did the Grand Prior with his battle; and the Duke of Alva with his son Don Fadrique, accompanied with divers others of great quality, seconded the battle in great march. Ludwig giving courage to his infantry, the base villains (as I showed you before) cried "*Geld, Geld,*" according to their simple and old base customs. Julián [Romero] and Robles being pell-mell with them, they hurled down their weapons, crying "Live Spaniard, bon papist moi." Notwithstanding, Ludwig recovered his horsemen, who began also to shake and to cry for money. True it is, at the first approach of the Duke of Alva in Friesland four days before, the horsemen began to murmur and to counsel Ludwig to return to Emden.

Ludwig, seeing this disaster, pulled off his casque, desiring his horsemen to follow him or to stand to bear witness how honestly his brother stood with some five hundred horsemen, desiring him to charge those lances which advanced hard before them. Count Adolf did it with great courage, although half his squadron quitted him. At which instant Ludwig cried to his horsemen, "All you that have a humor to live, follow me." Withal he gave the spurs. Some three hundred horsemen followed him; the rest ran away. Notwithstanding, his brother and himself with less than six hundred reiters drove about eight hundred lancers besides argoletiers into their vanguard of foot. By that time the Spanish general of horsemen was arrived with great troops, which soon mastered the Nassauians, in which place Ludwig was hurt very sore in two or three places, and his horse also. Notwithstanding, he escaped with wonderful hazard by swimming a river and recovered Emden. His brother, Count Adolf, with the most or all the gentlemen that followed him, were slain or taken, so that scarce forty escaped of both their troops. All or the most of his infantry were taken and slain, saving a troop which made a composition, being strongly entrenched with

27

Hendrik van Siegen. Notwithstanding, the Spanish used them cruelly according to their cowardly deserts, putting all or the most to the sword and winning all their artillery, munition, and baggage.

This overthrow recompensed double Ludwig's victory. But without doubt had the base people fought and followed Ludwig's directions, the loss had been the Spaniards', the seat of the Nassauians was such. Besides, I forget to speak of a ditch which Ludwig commanded to be cut in such sort that the water could have assured their quarter within less than ten hours. This valiant Count had reason to draw Vitelli to battle, knowing, in retiring before greater forces, the courage of his base soldiers would quail. But having intelligence of the Duke of Alva's approach, and finding the minds of his men failing, he had greater reason either to retire without engaging a fight or to have fortified a strong passage where he might have made head safely until the Prince his brother would have succored him with more supplies. This he might have done, considering the time and warning he had since the arrival of Vitelli until the coming of the Duke of Alva, principally since the overthrow of Arenberg, finding Groningen not to be taken and seeing forces increasing daily against him. But give him his worthy right. To correct his deeds I may be compared unto a counterfeit Alexander on a stage better than to the valiant and discreet Count.

℘

The Prince of Orange's first journey into Brabant

Touching the Prince of Orange's journey into Brabant, I can speak no more than this. By the aid of the Count Palatine of the Rhine and his own house of Nassau, which engaging the greatest part of his own country of Nassau, he levied some ten thousand reiters and twelve thousand landsknechts.[33] With those and some two thousand *ramassées* [34] of Walloons, French, and Flemings, fugitives, but a number of them brave gentlemen of good quality, especially the Count of Hohenlohe, being entered Cleveland, the Prince bent his course toward the river of Maas, resolving to pass the said river by the great and rich town of Liège, making account to find some good party in that town. Besides, divers of the other towns of Brabant, Flanders, and other provinces promised him assistance, in case he would encounter the Duke of Alva in the field.

Having passed the Maas, and being encamped by Liège, the Duke of Alva, understanding his meaning by good espials before his arrival, sent some captains of quality who were expert in those affairs both to the bishops and to the clergy to advertise and direct them to defend themselves, assuring them (if need required) he would hazard battle for them. This town, being neuter and of the Empire, only governed by priests and such men,[35] with the assistance and counsel of the Duke of Alva's instruments began to show themselves rather enemies than well-willers unto the Prince. Insomuch that divers sacked and spoiled some baggage and victuals loosely guarded which passed under their favors. The poor Prince, seeing himself so used by the Liègeois, was uncertain what to imagine, fearing the rest of the towns would do the like, having but small store of munition of his own and little hope to procure from others. Also the Duke of Alva fronted him with a fair army, but not comparable to his, especially in horsemen, for the Prince had more than double his numbers. Notwithstanding, the Duke of Alva was on the surest hand, by reason all the towns and passages were at his devotion.

[33] Infantry armed with pikes, trained to fight in masses.
[34] Troops scraped together.
[35] The See and city of Liège was a political as well as an ecclesiastical entity and was governed by a bishop.

Divers skirmishes passed betwixt both parties, but the Prince could never engage the Duke of Alva to battle, by reason he would be sure to be strongly entrenched (especially being in the field) and lodged often under the favor of his towns. Having intelligence that the Prince meant to enter Louvain to front him in his passage, he sent his great captain, Robles, and Mondragón, with some twenty ensigns of footmen, Spanish and Walloons, and five cornets of horsemen, into Tirlemont. This Tirlemont is within three leagues of Louvain, a place of no strength but sufficient to withstand the Prince's forces, having an army hard by to countenance them, for the Duke of Alva was encamped within three leagues.

In the Prince's march the garrison of Tirlemont annoyed him greatly, so that all his forces were constrained to stand in battle before Tirlemont until his rear guard and baggage were past. Insomuch that the Duke of Alva had the better means to look to Louvain; but, offering them garrison, they refused it, assuring him they would be loyal unto the King and him. The Duke of Alva politicly contented himself, fearing by despair to enforce them to revolt to the Prince. Notwithstanding, he used them with threatenings that he would look unto their doings, assuring them that he would account them rebels if they would assist the Prince with any necessaries,[36] but he doubted not their loyalties in defending the town.

To be the better assured, he sent divers of good judgment to assist and counsel them, as he did to Liège. Himself retired with his army near unto Brussels, to assure both Brussels and Mons in Hainaut. The Prince, being encamped under Louvain, found not them so angry as the priests of Liège, for Louvain was an university governed by good-natured people, and a number of nobility (as strangers term all gentlemen) were allied to the Prince or to divers of his followers. Besides, at that time the people in general hated the Spanish deadly, in such

[36] I.e., supplies.

sort that for all the Duke of Alva's instruments (but for their buttered hearts and phlegmatic livers) they would have opened their gates.

The Prince, perceiving their peevishness, seeing his orators could not prevail to make him enter, he burned their barriers and terrified them in such sort that either fear or love made them to give a great piece of money with much victuals. Perceiving his fortune, that no place would accept him and that the Duke of Alva would adventure no battle, he thought it his best to retire, but politicly he and his instruments persuaded their army that the Admiral Châtillon [37] was arrived in the frontiers of Artois with a mighty army of Frenchmen and that they would join with them. They gave out also that the Queen of England had sent a great treasure unto the Admiral to pay both their forces. Hereby they encouraged the mechanic mercenary reiters to march, having intelligence at Valenciennes, a town in Hainaut near unto the frontiers. Being arrived there, the Prince and his army began to take courage, partly because they knew the Duke of Alva would follow them no further, but chiefly because they might be presently in France; and although the army should mutiny according to their custom, as I said before, the Prince and his commanders might easily escape and shift for themselves, who otherwise should be in great danger; for, being engaged amongst their enemies, they might have been delivered by their own soldiers to the Duke of Alva either for passage or for money.

In this place the Prince, finding his reiters alert (as the Italians say) with advice of his valiant brother, he sent his trumpets to the Duke of Alva to tell him that he would be the next day four leagues toward him with fewer in number than himself did lead, where he would stay his answer and dare him battle. The Duke lay entrenched within six leagues of the Prince, having with him some twenty thousand. True it is his horsemen

[37] I.e., Admiral Gaspard de Coligny.

did not amount to four thousand, but they were Italians, Walloons, and Albanese, who in troth were to be valued with thrice as many reiters, yea, in my judgment with six times so many, being not accompanied with such chiefs as Count Ludwig. The trumpets being arrived, the Duke of Alva hanged one and answered the other:

Well, tell thy master my master will maintain his army continually, and thy master (I am assured) will break his within few days upon wants.[38] Therefore I have no reason to fight were I sure to win the battle. And although I know the valor of my men far surmounting his, yet, notwithstanding, no battle can be fought without some losses on both sides. For these causes I will not fight.

Vitelli persuaded him all he could to accept the offer and to fight, alleging the danger not to be great considering the difference betwixt the men, alleging also that in defeating the Prince and leaving his person dead in the field their wars would be ended by all reason. For my part I am of Vitelli's mind, but the wisest and of best judgment will be of the Duke of Alva's, for all battles end as pleaseth the great God. Had the Duke of Alva been defeated, he had not only lost his forces but all his master's countries.

The next day the Prince rose from Valenciennes according to promise, leaving all his baggage and worst-disposed soldiers in safety by Valenciennes. He marched with all or the most of his horsemen and footmen triumphing with drums and trumpets toward the Duke of Alva to the place his trumpets did assign. The Duke of Alva was also in order of battle but kept all his footmen in trenches with his horsemen, saving the guards which were beaten in by the valiant Count Ludwig, who led the vanguard with three thousand of the best sort of reiters. But the Prince and Mandelsloo, his marshal, with divers others, would not march so fast as Ludwig, with the battle [39] and rear guard.

[38] For lack of supplies.   [39] The main body of troops.

Wherefore Ludwig was forced to retire, being within sight of the Duke of Alva's trenches, raging with the Prince and the rest for not marching to force the trenches, alleging unto them, as it was very true, it were better to be defeated in fighting than for wants, as they were sure in a short time to be.

Being retired, they resolved to follow their first determination, the sooner the better, seeing Valenciennes would do nothing for them. The Duke of Alva, having news of their retreat and resolution, rose also, following them afar off like a fox, in such sort that he would be surely lodged and march safely from hazarding battle by Peronne on the French frontiers. Vitelli overtook divers baggages and stragglers in such sort that he put a number of them to the sword who were not guarded, by reason of their own negligence in straggling behind and aside the rear guard, unknown to Count Ludwig, who made the retreat. But so soon as Ludwig had knowledge hereof he returned in such sort that Vitelli and his vanguard of horsemen were forced to run till he met the Duke of Alva, to his disgrace, considering his speeches four days before. After this the Duke pursued no further, and the Prince and his army entered France, having no means to content his army but with spoils of the French, which they did not spare (as the provinces of Champagne and Picardy can witness) in their retreat to Germany.

This was the fortune of the poor Prince, for want of means to nourish his men of war, and will be of all others unless their chiefs provide in time either money or spoils. To say troth, the Prince's fortune might easily have been judged when he feared to enter Liège, for all voluntary armies, I mean that are not paid, are gone and defeated in short time in case they miss rich spoils at their first entry into the enemy's countries. In my time I remember four came to ruin with those fortunes. Besides this, they did some other matters about Zutphen, Roermond, and those parts, by means of the Prince's brother-in-law, the Count van den Bergh; but it proved to small effect, for always the masters of the field command all weak places in a short time. Wherefore (as I said before) a voluntary army must either be enriched presently with spoils or else assured by strong seats. But let the seat be never so strong, the master of the field will command it in time, unless it be some strong port like Flushing, La Rochelle, Calais, Marseilles, Brouage, Gravelines, or at the least some frontier strong place that a state or potentate dares not assiege, having no hope to despair the governor to deliver it into their enemy's hands. For example, Gourdan of Calais, being wooed and desired by his master the French king to deliver Calais unto his favorite Espernon, for all his fair words and large offers he would be governor still. So likewise Saint Luc held Brouage; also La Motte kept Gravelines, making his peace as pleased him with the Spanish king and after offending to the highest degree. Wherefore in a troubled estate there can be no surety comparable to a strong government.

೪

The Duke of Alva abuseth his master's service in not finishing the citadel of Flushing before that of Antwerp, and in neglecting to place sure garrisons in the seaports

After this the poor Prince remained in Germany (God knows), almost despairing to do any more good against the Spanish but that the Almighty stirred new instruments to maintain his cause and blinded the Spanish in their affairs. As I said before, they left the citadel of Flushing, being the only port and key of the Netherlands, unfinished, and ended that of Antwerp. All men of war of any judgment may easily conceive had they finished first the citadel of Flushing, Zeeland had never revolted. Yes, had they placed some two thousand soldiers in garrison in their ports of Brielle, Medemblik, and Haarlem, with some five hundred in the citadel of Flushing, Holland

and Friesland, with the rest of the province, had been sure; for the Spanish with their infinite Indian treasure, beside the rich Netherlands and other places, were sure to be masters of the field, having none to fear or to annoy them but England, Scotland, Germany, and France. Touching England, we had neither reason nor surety to have meddled with their actions without being assured of some of their best ports, the mutability of the people is such. Touching Scotland, I persuade myself they would not have meddled with them in case they had not been joined with England. Touching France, you saw the Spaniard's means so great in those parts that his faction was to be compared to the King's or any other and would have been far greater if the Guise had lived. Touching Germany, their house of Austria compassed the contrary of the best sort in those parts. As for mercenaries, we know it by good experience, commonly they follow the best purse, and by that reason the multitude of that nation [40] and Switzers had been theirs. Touching the state of Italy, either it is his or dare not offend him. For the Venetians are nobody without mercenaries. The Genoese are all or the most part at his devotion. The great houses of Mantua, Ferrara, Parma, Urbino, Grafino, with all the rest of any quality of those stirring spirits, are either his servants or pensioners. Touching the clergy, either his love or fear makes popes and cardinals as pleaseth him. Portugal is his. Touching Denmark, Sweden, the Hansa towns, Poland, and suchlike, they are either mercenaries too far off to annoy them or the most of them mechanics, without chiefs of any conduct.

Being assured (as they thought) of the Netherlanders' affairs, the Duke of Alva made his statue in brass, placed it in the midst of the castle of Antwerp, treading on the Counts of Egmond and Hoorne, with the Prince of Orange looking under him for ways to escape. He made also pieces of arras wherein were represented his sieges, battles, and actions of arms in one

[40] Germany.

piece, his own portraiture standing like the picture of the sun, with all the ensigns and cornets [41] which ever he won placed round about him.

℘

Count Ludwig surpriseth Mons in Hainaut, which is besieged and taken by the Duke of Alva

At this time the French king and they of the religion were at peace, so that the Admiral Châtillon thought himself assured of the King, but, poor lord, himself and many others were treacherously handled, as the Massacre of Paris can witness.

At this time Count Ludwig was in Paris and, finding access to the King by the Admiral's means, procured divers principals of the religion to promise to succor the Prince his brother and him against the Spanish, to whose demands the King agreed most willingly, by his Machiavellian mother's counsel,[42] who never cared what became of any estate or world to come so she might serve the present purpose and maintain her own greatness. Considering her Machiavellian humors, she was much to blame in this, knowing the French disposition rather than to live long in peace to fall into fight one with another. In going with Count Ludwig, she was assured that most or all which would go with him would be of the religion. If they prospered, Ludwig promised some frontier towns to the French for the King's use; if not, they might be glad to lose so many enemies.

By reason of the King's and his mother's dissembling leave, and Master Secretary Walsingham's true and honest meaning to the cause in general and to Count Ludwig in particular, the Count esteemed his affairs in good estate. Master Secretary, then being ambassador for the Queen's Majesty in Paris, fur-

[41] The battle flags which he had captured.
[42] Catherine de' Medici.

nished the Count all he could with countenance and crowns, in such sort that the Count resolved to depart into the Low Countries, having the Admiral's assurance to second him if his journey prospered. But presently there went with him Monsieur de la Noue, Monsieur de Poyet, Monsieur de Rouvray, Sir William Morgan, Monsieur Genlis, Monsieur de Mouy, with divers other French gentlemen of quality. These by the Admiral's means were to second him presently with six thousand footmen and some four hundred horse, all Frenchmen.

Count Ludwig sent sundry gentlemen Netherlanders, some known in Mons in Hainaut, some strangers unknown, appareled like merchants, who with their practice and means used the matter well with divers of the religion which were well known unto them, besides a number of papists, honest patriots who loved the Prince of Orange, principally because they knew that he and his hated the Spaniards. And although the Prince were of the religion, his promise was to grant liberty of conscience being victorious, for which cause he carried many thousand hearts more than he should have done otherwise. In those days few of the popular were of the religion, but all in general hated the Spanish deadly. Count Ludwig's instruments behaved themselves so well that promise was made unto them, when they would devise any means, they should be seconded to do the Prince service or any of his. This message being declared to the Prince, he returned the one party presently to their fellows whom they had left behind them in the town, giving them charge in the break of morning the third day to use the matter so that the porter should let them out at the ports of Havré. That being out, they should give the watch some bribe and shoot off a piece, appointing that he would be in person hard by ready to enter. According to promise, the parties executed his commandment, acquainting therewith an honest innkeeper of the religion.

The Count, giving order unto some seven hundred footmen

to march with all speed possible toward Mons, departed with the chiefs named before, accompanied with some four hundred brave horsemen, all or the most gentlemen and officers who had commanded before. The worst of these three, either La Noue, Poyet, or Rouvray, deserved to command twenty thousand men. The worthy Count, having made a great cavalcado [43] (as they term it) from his last lodging, arrived three hours before day at the place appointed. After leaving Messieurs de Poyet and Rouvray in ambush within four hundred paces of the port, himself, Monsieur de la Noue, Sir William Morgan, and some fifty horsemen approached as near unto the port as they could be covered. According unto promise the merchants were let out, and withal a piece went off, at which noise the Count and his troop rushed in, divers pieces and petronels [44] going off. The watchmen ran away at the noise; Messieurs de Poyet and Rouvray dislodged on the spur and entered also. The Count, entering the market place and there setting his men in order, caused all the magistrates to be assembled. Being together, he used these speeches:

Dear countrymen, my coming is not against you but against the tyrannous Spaniards, who have undone the Prince my brother and all his house and will make you slaves if you do not resolve to prevent them, which you may if it please you. Join with me, and I assure you I come not hither of myself but am promised by the French king and other potentates to be seconded presently. In the meantime you shall see Ludwig and his troops sufficient to answer the fury of the Duke of Alva. Assure yourselves, without the aid of mighty strangers and assurance that my brother the Prince will march with all speed to our succors with a puissant army, I and these gentlemen had never engaged ourselves upon any land town as this is. Although we need not to fear, knowing the strength of

[43] Cavalcade.
[44] A hand firearm introduced in the sixteenth century, shorter than the ordinary harquebus but longer than the pistol. A sort of large horse pistol.

the place to be sufficient to withstand any forces that shall present themselves before it, being manned with a reasonable troop, much more having so many chiefs as you see here,

naming unto him the great captains that accompanied him, whose names were well known unto most of the burgesses. His speeches gave great courage unto the burgesses, who were soon persuaded to depart peaceably to their houses and to deliver the keys of their gates to the Count.

Although the people hated the Spanish deadly, they knew not what to make of this surprise, whereat great murmuring was in corners. Some feared Ludwig would alter their Mass, which they most esteemed (for all or the most part were Roman Catholics). Others feared the Duke of Alva's fury, in such sort that many presented supplications to the Count that he would permit them to depart the town with their wealth and baggage. Some had leave, especially such as were known to be obstinately Spaniolized, who eased the rest greatly that stayed, for in their houses the Count lodged divers of his troops, and were for the most part the wealthiest of the town. The Duke of Alva, hearing this, was greatly amazed, although the French king advertised him how all promises passed in France and that he had made a draught for his master and himself to be quit of a great number of enemies, thinking indeed that Ludwig and all his followers should fall into his hands. But the Count himself and his vigilant followers deceived both King and Duke, who (as you heard) surprised Mons suddenly and unlooked for at both their hands. This made the Duke of Alva amazed, thinking the French king doubled with him and his master, as King Henry and his Constable, Montmorency, did for Metz in Lorraine with Charles the Fifth.

Count Ludwig's footmen (named before) being arrived, and the Count perceiving the murmur of the greatest part of the townsmen, who were very well armed, strong, and in good order (in such sort that the Duke of Alva, using before all the policy he could, never could place garrison in this town, by reason of their strong seat, well fortified, and above three thousand men bearing arms, besides as many or more able to carry arms, all obstinate, mutinous Walloons, wanting neither victuals, artillery, nor munition), he sought to make his party and himself as strong as he could. And hearing how the Duke of Alva gathered all the forces he could with great speed and preparations to besiege him presently, he acquainted therewith them of the religion and such burgesses as he thought assured unto him.

After placing his men in order in the market place and seizing on the best in Mons, he made proclamation upon pain of death that all townsmen should bring their arms into the townhouse within six hours, which was obeyed with all possible speed. This done, he gave arms unto some five hundred of the religion and assured unto him; the rest he fed with fair words, assuring them on his honor that neither himself nor any of his companies should abuse them. But what he did was for the surety of himself and his company, assuring them, if the siege presented not, to deliver them their arms again. If it presented, and it pleased the Almighty to favor him, at the enemy's retreat he would leave them as he found them, conditionally to accept a small garrison during the Spanish government. "As for such," said he, "as will not endure my government and orders, let them come unto me. They shall have free leave to depart with all their goods, leaving behind them victuals and such necessaries as may pleasure their besieged friends." They, seeing their fellows' houses who departed before used with havoc, which happened (as they thought) for want of masters to keep them and to complain of their guests' abuses, seeing also they could not carry away the one quarter of their goods, the most part resolved to stay, desiring the Count's leave to signify unto their friends in Antwerp and Brussels how they were constrained to stay perforce in the town, meaning by that means to excuse themselves unto the Duke of Alva, whom they feared above all the world.

Every day some of Ludwig's horsemen ran unto the ports [45] of Brussels and up and down the countries as pleased them, spoiling and wasting what they listed. Often they had great skirmishes, but always they defeated their enemies with half their numbers, in such sort that the Duke of Alva's captains made ambushes for them, five hundred at a time, and the others would pass through them, being scarce half their numbers. This continued some time, but Alva, having gathered his forces, dispatched Chiappino Vitelli with the most of his cavalry and certain regiments of footmen, giving him charge to enclose the town in such sort as the garrison could not sally forth.

Being approached Mons, Ludwig sallied, accompanied with the Lord of La Noue, and Poyet, Sir William Morgan, and divers other adventurers of good quality, with all his horsemen and half his footmen, leaving Monsieur de Rouvray in the town, well accompanied with the rest. Being passed his counterscarp,[46] he left Monsieur de la Noue, who gave order unto five hundred harquebusiers to hide themselves close in the highways and some hundred score [47] from the gates. Poyet and La Noue stood with two squadrons of horses a little before them, either squadron being of an hundred and fifty; the rest the Count commanded to go to engage the enemy to skirmish. Monsieur de Rouvray caused divers pieces of artillery to be transported from other mounts unto the mounts that commanded the field toward the enemy.

The enemy advanced bravely both horse and foot, at which sight Ludwig's couriers encountered theirs with sundry cornets,

[45] Gates.

[46] Of the ditch surrounding a fortified place, the sloping face of the ditch closest to the defenders was called the "escarp" and the sloping outer face of the ditch was called the "counterscarp."

[47] Two thousand paces.

but they forced the Nassauians to retire and double their paces toward La Noue and Poyet. At this sight La Noue advanced, desiring the Count to give order to Poyet to stand and the harquebusiers to keep close, telling him, "I know the enemy will repulse me. Notwithstanding, I will charge with your leave. In my retreat, let the ambush of shot discharge their volleys; then Poyet may charge the better cheap." [48] The couriers being hard at hand, La Noue advanced, crying to his company, "Courage! Turn bridle!" and withal, charging some four hundred lancers and argoletiers, gave them the retreat into our squadrons, which advanced to re-encounter La Noue, at whose sight La Noue retired, bringing the enemies full upon the ambush of shot, which gave them such a salvo of harquebuses that happy was he that retired first. Withal, Poyet charged very courageously, in such sort that the enemies doubled their paces toward their battle,[49] at whose retreat the Count wisely retired his footmen into the town with his horsemen in good order.

In the meantime Monsieur de Rouvray forgot not to plague them with his artillery. The general of the horsemen and Vitelli advanced; their battle remained, half of horse and foot in arms, until their quarters were entrenched, which they did in a short time, for they were furnished with a great number of pioneers and all necessaries; in such sort that in less than forty hours they assured the one half of the town from sallying forth. Notwithstanding, the ports toward Valenciennes and Havré were clear.

There stood an abbey or cloister some half an English mile from the town, on a little river which ran from the town to the cloister.[50] The place was not strong nor able to abide the can-

[48] More advantageously.   [49] Their main body.
[50] The abbey was called Espinleu. Emanuel van Meteren, *Belgica . . . Historie der Nederlandscher ende haerder na-buren Oologen ende Geschiedenissen, tot den Iare* M.VI^C. *XII* . . . (The Hague, 1623), folio 83 recto column 2, and 79 recto column 1.

non. Nevertheless it was necessary to be kept, for betwixt it and the town there was good store of grass and corn, with other necessaries to feed horses and cattle. Besides, they were assured the enemy would attempt this place first. Therefore to win time it was most necessary to be kept. Into this cloister Monsieur de Poyet desired to go with some eight hundred harquebusiers, although the Count and the rest were loath to hazard his person. Notwithstanding, the other, alleging himself to be but the third person in the town, desired and persuaded them that half their footmen should not go to keep any place without the company of a principal chief. To fulfill his desire it was granted him, referring all unto himself, being entreated not to engage himself further than he might well retire and assured that Ludwig and the rest would quit the town and all to follow him, although they were sure to perish.

Monsieur de Poyet, having possessed the place and furnished with about ten days' victuals, used all means to strengthen himself. By this time Vitelli had made the quarters toward Brussels very strong, in such sort that two thousand were sufficient to guard it against ten thousand. For he made there good forts about a quarter of a league one from another, with strong trenches that ran from fort to fort, that no horsemen could sally over them, and their footmen durst not pass those guards for fear of the Count's horsemen.

Vitelli dislodged with all his horse and foot, saving the guards which he left in his forts, and remained in battle betwixt the ports of Valenciennes and Havré until he erected a large fort like unto the others. Having left two regiments of footmen in it, he retired with his cavalry and the rest of his footmen unto the next village some half a league off, leaving near half his troops in guard that they might be sure until the arrival of the Duke of Alva, who began to set out from Brussels with the rest of his army, artillery, munition, and baggage that night about two hours before day. The town and cloister, having intelligence, sallied out from both quarters some eight hundred footmen with all their horsemen to give a camisado [51] under the conduct of Monsieur de Rouvray. Being met in one place, they gave furiously into Vitelli's quarter and forced his guards into their place of arms. Mendoza, being lodged apart with most of the cavalry, gathered presently his horsemen in order and gave resolutely into Vitelli's quarter, which was in danger to be run through with this camisado. Monsieur [de] Rouvray, like a discreet soldier, had left one of his best captains short of the enemy's quarter with some three hundred of his best shot and a hundred and fifty horsemen for his retreat, which saved him and the most of his troops. Mendoza charged Rouvray in such sort that happy was he who could return first. Coming unto his ambush, they peppered Mendoza and his horsemen with a salvo of harquebuses that turned them back upon the other, at which instant the hundred and fifty horsemen charged them on their backs. By that time Vitelli and the most of his troops were in order, advancing with all speed toward Rouvray's. Notwithstanding, Rouvray and his brave captains (especially his cavalry) retired with small loss into the cloister, where Poyet was ready to receive them in order without, in such sort that Vitelli pursued no further. At this camisado the enemy lost six for one of the Nassauians, by reason Rouvray had forced their guards before the rest were in arms.

The next day toward night the Duke of Alva's vanguard was in sight of the town, but before his rear guard came to their quarter it was nine of the clock the next morning, by reason they marched very slowly, and not without reason, for they haled with them two-and-twenty pieces of battery, besides some other fieldpieces with all the munition belonging unto them. The Duke of Alva, being arrived, encamped on the riverside betwixt the meadows and the hills from the ways toward Va-

[51] A surprise attack either during the night or at break of day in which the attackers wore shirts over their armor for mutual recognition.

lenciennes down to the cloister. Along this river he made strong trenches which assured his army toward the fields. Toward the town he made large deep trenches impossible to be entered. This man would commonly assure himself with trenches although the enemies were lodged three days' journey from him. Now before Mons he entrenched all his quarters as though he meant to be besieged, and not without reason, having intelligence how Monsieur Genlis marched for their succors with seven thousand Frenchmen and the Prince of Orange making ready a mighty army in Germany.

After his arrival, the next day, he prepared to beat the cloister, unto which place he brought six pieces of cannon. Monsieur de Poyet resolved before not to keep the place but to win time in forcing them to place the cannon. This cloister was so near the town that none could encamp betwixt it and the town, by reason of the town's artillery and of wet meadow grounds which could not be entrenched. Wherefore Monsieur de Poyet did most bravely abide this whole day's battery and in the night set the cloister on fire with a train, and so retired himself and his troops safely into the town, leaving nothing behind.

Within few days the Duke of Alva began to make his approaches, in such sort that he assured the town from sallying (saving their secret sallies through the rampire and bulwarks) before he mounted his pieces to beat the forts and defenses. The town plagued him greatly with their counterbattery, and besides they often sallied and annoyed them with sundry attempts on their artillery and trenches. With much ado, after receiving great losses, he made three platforms. The midst did batter the port of Havré, the two others the flanks and parts of the curtains [52] on both sides. On these three platforms he placed two-and-twenty cannons, with which and with his culverins that did beat the defenses he discharged during his siege above twenty-

[52] The parts of the rampart between two bastions, or towers, or gates. Here it refers to the wall on either side of the Havré gate.

four thousand shot. The fury of all batteries are past at the first, I mean within two days, yea, commonly in one; for the defendants, knowing the place and the success of the fury, will reinforce their breaches and re-entrench themselves in such sort that the assailants can do small hurt with their approaches. The second day they battered, and having made their breach reasonable (as they thought) they prepared to the assault. The point [53] fell by lot to the Tercio of Lombardy, led by the valiant monsieur of the camp,[54] Julián Romero, who was seconded by the master of the camp, Don Francisco de Valdéz and his Tercio de la Ligue, after him the regiments of Walloons of the Marquis of Havré, Count Berlaymont, Messieurs de Licques and of Capres. So were all the rest of the army in battle ready to second one another according to their direction, with their whole cavalry in order of battle, some quarter of a league from their trenches. Divers had leave to dismount themselves, who accompanied Julián [Romero] at the point. The Count re-entrenched himself overthwart the breach with a half-moon.[55] Himself and some two hundred horsemen stood at the mouth of the great lane toward the breach. The rest of his horsemen were in three troops making patrols ("rounds" we call it) from place to place round about the town. As one troop came unto him, he sent another out. Monsieur de la Noue stood with the armed men [56] in the midst of the half-moon. Monsieur de Poyet stood on the one quarter of the moon with half the shot, Monsieur de Rouvray on the other with the rest. At every corner of the moon they placed divers pieces of ordnance laden with nails, small bullets, and stones, which flanked the mouth of the breach. Julián's captains would not give place one to another more than

[53] The advanced position.

[54] Monsieur of the camp is Williams' rendering of *maestre de campo,* an officer equivalent in rank to a colonel.

[55] That is, the defender made a semicircle of trenches around the breach which had been made in the wall of the town.

[56] Men in armor.

the colonels but by lot. After knowing who should lead and the breach discovered saultable,[57] Julián commanded the point to the assault, which were suffered to enter; but being in the midst of the moon they were murdered like dogs, in such sort that happy was he that could retire first. Notwithstanding, Julián advanced with all courage with his seconds, but, being on the breach and having discovered their trenches and works within, he caused his troops to retire, not without loss, for all their small shot played incessantly upon his troops. At this assault the Spaniards' courage was quailed from assaulting any more. Julián escaped with great danger, having sundry harquebuses on his arms.[58] His lieutenant colonel was slain with five of his principal captains and the bravest part of his soldiers, besides many adventurers as well horsemen as footmen which were not of his regiment. The Count escaped not freely, for divers of his best men were slain, especially Monsieur de Rouvray shot in the head with a musket. The Duke of Alva, perceiving the valor and conduct of Ludwig and his men, resolved not to force his breach but cunningly attempted them often with alarms and counterfeit assaults, in such sort that he spoiled many of the defendants with his artillery in presenting themselves on the breach.

At this instant Monsieur Genlis was marching with his succors in number (as I said before) seven thousand French, all footmen, saving some four hundred horsemen. Being arrived hard by Valenciennes, the Duke of Alva sent Don Fadrique with his marshal, Chiappino Vitelli, accompanied with 1,500 horsemen and 4,000 footmen; himself remained in strong trenches with all the rest in arms, who being all together were about one-and-twenty thousand footmen and three thousand horsemen. Monsieur Genlis, although he was a most gallant soldier, at this re-encounter showed small discipline, Vitelli having intelligence of his march and order.

Don Fadrique being arrived at Saint-Ghislain some two

---

[57] Assaultable. [58] His armor was hit by shots.

leagues from Mons, hearing Genlis was in march and that he meant to pass that way within ten hours, Vitelli desired him to leave all his men in ambush in that place in troops on both sides of the highways. Having finished his orders, he commanded his nephew, Juan Bautista del Monte, lieutenant general of the horsemen, to march with five hundred horsemen, half lancers, the rest argoletiers, giving him in charge to march in three troops softly until his couriers should meet his enemies, then to return one troop after another without engaging himself to fight unless the enemy would enforce him, but to use all means to bring them engaged unto the ambush, then to run with his troops as though he were afraid, aside of the ambush. He was not two leagues from Vitelli, but his couriers met the French, who, according to their accustomed fury, charged the Spanish couriers, and they, according to their direction, retired before them; so did their second, and Bautista himself with the third, bringing them in his tail unto the place directed. By this time all or the most of the French horsemen were arrived, charging Bautista his troops who could first, persuading themselves all to be theirs. Vitelli, like a discreet captain, desired Don Fadrique to suffer them to run until they were entered into the ambush of five hundred musketeers which stood under a hedge where they must pass and, being entered, to charge them with half the horsemen, which stood equally divided on both sides of the way. By that time the French were entered the ambush of musketeers, and perceiving the squadrons of lancers advancing toward them, they began to retire and to double their paces back, but withal, Don Fadrique charged. Juan Bautista, being on the other side, turned also. So did Vitelli second with the rest, in such sort that presently their few horsemen were forced to run through their own footmen, which brake in a short time, for they marched far asunder (as they said) two leagues from their first troops unto their last. Besides, they had no companies of pikes to make any stand, especially their horsemen being broken. Monsieur de Mouy escaped into Mons by reason of the woodland countries. Few returned into France, because the peasants murdered them in cold blood. After the overthrow the greatest part of them were executed. Monsieur Genlis with divers gentlemen resisted valiantly, but at the last he was mastered and carried prisoner into the castle of Antwerp, where himself and an English gentleman taken with him named Master John Winkfield were executed long afterwards.

The Duke of Alva, hearing that the Prince of Orange was ready to march with ten thousand reiters and twelve thousand landsknechts besides divers fugitive Netherlanders, commanded his officers to strengthen his trenches with all speed, as well toward the town as the field, giving order that all the munition and victuals that might be gotten should be brought into his camp and that his horsemen should bring in all the forage they could and spoil the rest. For he resolved to stay in the field and at least to famish either the Prince or the town, giving charge unto all men not to engage any skirmish or fight but to make the town from sallying forth.

The Prince arrived with his army mentioned before, without any let [59] to speak of until he encamped on the top of the hills toward Valenciennes within half a league of the Duke of Alva's trenches, at whose sight the Duke gave strait charge that none should sally out of his trenches, giving the Prince leave to encamp quietly without skirmishing. That night the Prince sent often divers troops unto the Duke's trenches, thinking to keep his army in arms, but none seemed to stir or to take an alarm. The next morning the Prince sent great troops of horse and foot to procure the enemy to sally, standing himself with the rest in order of battle in sight of the town and of the Duke of Alva; but none would sally out of the trenches, in such sort that the Prince dislodged [60] with his whole forces, resolving to force their

[59] I.e., hindrance.   [60] Moved, shifted position.

trenches or to lose not a few of his best men. Being in order of battle near unto the Duke of Alva, he sent his marshal, Mandelsloo, with three thousand landsknechts and three thousand reiters, giving them order to charge the trenches with all resolution. Being approached within musket shot of the Spanish and Walloons, the poor Almans' courage began to quail, not without reason, finding better shot than themselves within the trenches and their horsemen not serviceable, upon whom all their glory did rest. Notwithstanding that Mandelsloo and his troops began to retire, the Lord of Druynen, the Prince's lieutenant, and Count Hohenlohe, with divers others of quality accompanied with many troops of horse and foot, marched resolutely and attempted the trenches against reason, for, receiving hot salvos of musketadoes,[61] they were forced to retire; at which attempt the Lord of Druynen was slain with divers others of quality and a great number of their soldiers both horse and foot.

The Prince being retired into his camp, Julián Romero with earnest persuasions procured license of the Duke of Alva to hazard a camisado that night upon the Prince. At midnight Julián sallied out of the trenches with a thousand musketeers and two thousand armed men, most pikes. All the rest stood in arms in the trenches, their horsemen ready without the trenches to second Julián, principally for his retreat if need were. Julián divided his forces into three troops: the first two hundred, old shot which could keep their matches close, led by a desperate captain named Muxica; the second one thousand armed men and shot led by Julián himself; the third led by his lieutenant colonel and sergeant major, whom he commanded to stand fast in the midst of their way betwixt the two camps for his retreat and not to stir unless some of credit came from him to command the contrary. Presently, after his directions, he commanded Muxica to charge, who resolutely forced two guards, being at the least

---

[61] Musket shot.

a regiment of Almains.[62] Julián seconded with all resolution in such sort that he forced all the guards that he found in his way into the place of arms [63] before the Prince's tent. Here he entered divers tents; amongst the rest his men killed two of the Prince's secretaries hard by the Prince's tent; and the Prince himself escaped very narrowly, for I heard the Prince say often that, as he thought, but for a dog he had been taken. The camisado was given with such resolution that the place of arms took no alarm until their fellows were running in with the enemies in their tails, whereupon this dog, hearing a great noise, fell to scratching and crying and withal leapt on the Prince's face, awaking him, being asleep, before any of his men. And albeit the Prince lay in his arms with a lackey always holding one of his horse ready bridled, yet, at the going out of his tent, with much ado he recovered his horse before the enemy arrived. Nevertheless, one of his equerries was slain taking horse presently after him, and divers of his servants were forced to escape amongst the guards of foot which could not recover their horses. For troth, ever since, until the Prince's dying day, he kept one of that dog's race; so did many of his friends and followers. The most or all of these dogs were white little hounds with crooked noses called camuses.

The camp, being in arms and in some order, made head toward Julián in such sort that he commanded the retreat. Before he could recover his stand with his lieutenant, the army began to charge him in great troops, in such sort that with much ado he could arrive with his troops, and for all his good order he lost many of his men as well taken as slain. Having recovered

[62] Variant of Almans, Germans.
[63] The phrase has several meanings. Here it means the open space near the center of the camp where the guard might be assembled or a review held. Here also, as is obvious from the text, were the tents of the principal officers.

his stand with the presence of the two thousand horsemen which came for his retreat, the Nassauians followed no further.

Without doubt had the Duke of Alva followed Julián's counsel the Prince had been defeated in that place. Julián advised that all their horsemen and half their footmen should have been in a stand where he left his lieutenant, and himself with his three thousand to enter the Prince's camp; that having good success, the stand should have entered also. For my part I am of Julián's mind, but the wisest sort are of the Duke of Alva's. Although Julián's courage assured him victory, the Duke of Alva had reason not to hazard his forces in battle, being assured the Prince would be forced to retire with wants. For if the Prince and his army had been in arms and in order it must have sorted to a battle, having made half his army to run, and perhaps by that means the Prince might have succored the town. For, without doubt, let two armies encamp, one hard by another, the first that discountenanceth his fellow is in great hope of victory, or at least by all reasons to make his adversary to retire.

This camisado quailed the poor Almains in such sort that the Prince was glad to use all the policy he could to retire, thinking the sooner the better, for fear lest his reiters would grow to their old custom to cry for *geld* which he had not. To prevent all mutinies, he caused his officers and many of his best instruments to give forth that his brother Count John was arrived with five hundred reiters by Roermond and with great treasure (sufficient to pay all his forces for three months) from the Queen's Majesty, the King of Denmark, and the German princes of the religion. His camp being thoroughly furnished with these speeches, he dislodged the next day, making all the haste he could to recover the Maas. Withal he advertised his brother of his fortune, desiring him to make the best shift for himself that he could.

The Prince, being arrived by Roermond, having intelligence with divers towns in Holland, fed his army with good speeches, assuring them that his brother Count John was at 's Heerenberg with his brother-in-law, Count van den Bergh, and that he would send for them to make his passage over the Maas where his brother Count Ludwig would arrive, whom he looked for daily to come from Mons.

After the Prince's retreat, Count Ludwig, finding no remedy, began to parley, but stood on most honorable terms. The Duke of Alva, knowing him to be a most honorable resolute man and the town not to be taken by fury, fearing delays would grow to disadvantage, accepted his parley, agreeing to such conditions as pleased the Count, in such sort that Ludwig and his garrison was to pass over the river of Maas where his brother the Prince was staying for him. Being met, resolution was taken that Ludwig should pass into Germany and the Prince into Holland. The Prince, fearing the worst, passed the river by night with a few gentlemen; amongst others Sir William Morgan was one. The Prince's sudden departure gave a great murmuring amongst the reiters. Notwithstanding, he wrote a letter to his brother to assure him that he would content them with all speed possible and that his going into Holland was principally to seek means to pay them, giving to his brother leave and authority to sell all that he had in Germany rather than he should be disgraced with false promises. This letter, being read openly, gave some contentment unto the army, but principally the person of Count Ludwig stayed them, whom they much honored and respected, knowing no fault to be in him.

I forgot to write how Malines accepted a garrison of the Prince, as some of his forces passed by it in going to Mons, which afterwards retired with the Prince. The Duke of Alva, for their reward after the taking of Mons, sent his master of the camp, Julián Romero, with his Tercio of Lombardy and others, who entered the town and sacked it to the uttermost.

The beginning and ending of this siege was most honorable although unfortunate. Sometimes great captains wrong themselves. Had the Count left either Monsieur de la Noue, or Monsieur de Rouvray, or Monsieur de Poyet Governor in Mons, and retired himself with the other to prepare their succors, by all reason it had been far better, for the least of the three had been sufficient to command the town and the two others would have stood the succors in good stead, I mean the Prince and Monsieur Genlis. The only way for the Prince had been to have encamped before Brussels, which was a weak rich town, unfortified, where he must have forced the Duke of Alva either to leave his siege to fight with him or else to lose the town, and not to attempt trenches which wanted no defense that could be desired. Touching Monsieur Genlis, the world may judge there might have been better order at his defeat.

❦

The revolt of Flushing, the brave resolution of Worst, the seaman, and of the Baily, Monsieur de Baerland, in seizing on the town and in executing Señor Pacheco

During the siege of Mons, one Señor Pacheco came from the Duke of Alva with a commission to be Governor of Flushing and of the Rammekens. Pacheco had also authority to execute divers of the inhabitants in Flushing, principally the Baily, Monsieur de Baerland, and Worst, the famous seaman. At this instant they began the citadel of Flushing. Pacheco, being let in with some of his fellows, and the rest at the gates having intelligence with Monsieur de Beauvoir, Governor of Middelburg, thought within three days to have placed a garrison of Spaniards and Walloons in Flushing and then to have finished the rest of his purposes at pleasure. Worst began to mistrust the matter. Whereupon he went to Monsieur de Baerland, telling him resolutely that he would not stand to the Spanish government nor trust to their courtesies. Monsieur de Baerland began to lean to his opinion and to apprehend some fear, because he had received divers letters from his friends in Brabant that Pacheco would come to be Governor of Flushing and that the Duke of Alva was informed of some matters against Baerland and the said Worst, with divers others. Hereupon Monsieur de Baerland and Worst resolved to lay hands on Pacheco and to seize upon the town. Being respected and greatly beloved of the popular, they made divers acquainted with the Duke of Alva's practices and how Pacheco was the man that should execute his determination. Presently they gave order to make good watch at the water-port to prevent the entry of the Spaniards, who were hard by it with their arms in their hands, ready to enter. Withal they assembled all the magistrates and burgesses into their townhouse, whither they sent for Pacheco, making him believe they would obey all his directions, conditionally that he would show them his authority. Pacheco being arrived amongst them, Monsieur de Baerland asked him for his commission. Pacheco showed it. Withal Worst laid hands on him saying, "Shellum [64] Spaniard, thou hast more directions than these." Pacheco striving with Worst, Worst and his companions threw him down, giving him and his followers store of good blows. Rifling Pacheco, they found about him all his directions, whereby divers of them were to be executed. Presently they carried Señor Pacheco to the gallows, where they hung the Duke of Alva's scutcheon, at which they hanged Pacheco with his commission about his neck, although Pacheco offered them assurance of ten thousand ducats to have his head struck off. They hanged also some five-and-twenty of his followers, beating them with stones and cudgels all the way as they passed to the gallows. Monsieur de Beauvoir arrived at the gates toward Middelburg with some four hundred Walloons within two hours after the executing of Pacheco. The Flushingers resolved to re-

[64] A rogue, a rascal, a worthless fellow.

sist his entry. Beauvoir, being a white-livered soldier, retired into Middelburg.

Without doubt, had he showed any valor, he might have entered, for at that instant Flushing was nothing fortified to speak of, saving toward the water. The rest was a low green rampire without flanks,[65] parapet, or ditch (but such as men of any resolution might have entered), or any pieces mounted toward the land, unless it were some paltry rusty old clinks [66] which a man would as readily choose in a manner to stand before as behind at their going off. Presently the Flushingers fell to working night and day on their rampire and drew divers pieces of ordnance out of their ships and mounted them thereon. They dispatched also letters into England and France for succors with a few crowns. Flushing was in those days (God knows) a poor beggarly town of fishing in respect of that it is now, without town, fort, fortress, or village to friend in all that country.

As God would, there were divers followers of the Prince of Orange and of his brother Count Ludwig. Some were seamen, named by the enemies "freebooters," but some of them were resolute gallant gentlemen, namely De Lumbres, Schoonewal, Bartel Entens van Mentheda, Ruychaver, and so forth. These were sea captains, roving out of their countries where fortune served them best, in the Prince of Orange's name. There were also divers Walloons and Flemings which kept the woods of Flanders, not knowing how to escape, namely the Captains Bernaert, Eloy, Ambroise le Duc, and others. Hearing of the revolt of Flushing, they marched directly thither and at a place named Nieuwehaven [67] they made a strong trench, in which place they remained not three days but the Flushingers sent their boats to fetch them. The Captains Bernaert, Eloy, and Am-

---

[65] Generally speaking, in fortifications any part of a work that defends another work along the outside of the parapet.

[66] Worn cannon.

[67] A bay on the western Scheldt to the east of Breskens.

broise le Duc, being entered Flushing with some four hundred
Walloons and Flemings well armed, did something assure the
town. Some of these had good understanding in the wars. Principally in fortification they did help the townsmen greatly, in
such sort that they mounted their pieces in good order and
mended their fortifications.

ॐ

*Captain Thomas Morgan comes to Flushing, which was
the first English band that served the Netherlanders
against the Spanish king*

At this time there was a fair muster of Londoners before the
Queen's Majesty at Greenwich. Amongst the Londoners were
divers captains and soldiers who had served some in Scotland,
some in Ireland, others in France. And having nothing to do,
with the countenance of some great men who favored the cause
and the small helps of the deputies of Flushing, Captain
Thomas Morgan levied a fair company of three hundred strong,
amongst whom were divers officers which had commanded
before, with many gentlemen, at the least above one hundred,
amongst which myself was one. This band was the first that
served the Netherlanders, I mean since the Duke of Alva came
to be Governor and Captain General of the Netherlands.

Captain Morgan and his company arrived in good time, for
at his arrival Flushing was in distress. For the Duke of Alva
had sent forces of Walloons and Spaniards under the conduct
of Don Ruffello to second Monsieur de Beauvoir, who had command to entrench themselves on the dike toward the Rammekens. Had they done it, the town could not have cut the ditch,
as they did afterwards, and the Duke of Alva was to second
them with all his whole forces. But hearing how the English
were arrived in greater numbers than we were indeed, the

57

Duke of Alva stayed to march in good order and with great
means, for he wanted a number of sea provisions. Also Beauvoir and Ruffello, hearing of our arrival, made no haste to march.

In the meantime there arrived from La Rochelle three fair
companies led by the Captains Henri, Tristan, and Vitran, of
which one was levied for Monsieur Tseraerts, who was appointed Governor of Flushing by letters from the Prince of Orange. These troops being arrived, we thought ourselves assured
in the town. Belike the Duke of Alva was offended with Beauvoir
and Ruffello, not without reason, for no two captains could do
their general worse service than they did; for without doubt
they might have lodged on the ditch before the arrival of Captain Morgan, besides the cowardliness of Beauvoir for not forcing the town when Pacheco arrived. Perceiving the Duke of
Alva to be in choler, they (to repair their fault) resolved to attempt the ditch. And to do it the better, they thought good to
mount certain culverins on a forced hill (I mean made with
men's hands) which stood some half a mile from the town betwixt the way of Middelburg and the dike, I mean the fourth
dike from Flushing to Middelburg. Beauvoir kept some two
hundred Walloons in a strong house, halfway betwixt Middelburg and Flushing. This place was guardable without battery.
Into this place Beauvoir and Ruffello brought their forces,
which might be some twenty-five hundred Spaniards and Walloons. Out of that place they advanced at midnight, leaving
their great troop hidden out of the highway within a quarter
of a mile of the said hill. At the break of day they sent some
hundred shot toward the hill.

The garrison, perceiving their meaning, sallied with about
seven hundred English, French, and Walloons, who were desired and commanded by Tseraerts to dig down the hill. According to direction the garrison advanced and, being approached, the enemy retired. Our men being at work, the enemy advanced some four hundred shot, which entered into hot

skirmish. Ours followed them so fast that their ambush was fain to discover themselves for their safeguard, at whose sight ours retired in good order by reason half our men made a stand for the retreat of those which charged. After this skirmish Tseraerts, discovering the number of enemies, retired the garrison into the town, not without reason, for he thought he marched to besiege us and knew no other but that the most of their army might be at Middelburg or thereabouts.

Our men so behaved themselves at this skirmish that the enemy lost three for one, notwithstanding the enemy tarried in the place and after dinner made as though they would take the hill. The morning skirmish liked our captains so well as they desired the Governor's leave to sally, which earnest request was granted upon condition not to engage themselves too far. Whereupon the Governor and the captains mounted on the rampire to direct their fight. Having resolved, Captain Morgan and our Englishmen had the vanguard. To make the skirmish the more honorable, we sallied with our ensigns; [68] the Frenchmen were to second us, the Walloons and Flemings last. The whole were in number some eight hundred.

Captain Morgan, being arrived within a great musket shot from the enemy, made a stand [69] and advanced his shot forwards, giving them commandment to stand also until he commanded them or the enemy forced them. He placed his armed men on both sides of the bridge, leaving a ditch betwixt them and the enemy, and stood himself with a troop of gentlemen on the causeway before the bridge. The two troops of Frenchmen and Walloons placed themselves in meadows on both sides of the causeway, leaving their few armed men right against Captain Morgan. They placed their shot in ditches, a little before their armed men, saving some one hundred whom they directed to enter into skirmish when the English began.

Our order was scarce directed but the enemy charged our

[68] Here the word means battle flags.   [69] Halted the troops.

men very hotly, in such sort that all or the most part of both parties' shot were by the ears. Notwithstanding that theirs were twice so many, ours quit themselves very valiantly, until a great squadron of their armed men advanced, which forced our English shot to retire, by reason that most of the English shot skirmished on the causeway and hard by it on both sides where the enemies could join with them. At this sight Captain Morgan and his armed men advanced resolutely to the push of the pike,[70] and so did the French and Walloons' shot flank amongst them their volleys [71] that they plagued them greatly; in such sort that the enemy advanced no further. To say troth, they could not join with ours, by reason ours kept the ditches and bridge. Perceiving they could not force our quarter, the enemy retired but stood fast within a great musket shot of the place. Tseraerts, perceiving the enemy's mind, thinking they would charge again, and fearing we had lost more than we did, sent unto ours to retire, which they did with good order into the town, with small loss in respect of the skirmish, which endured very hot and almost the space of two hours, in which time our men came twice to the push of the pike.

Once the enemy had hold on Captain Morgan's ancient,[72] which was rescued bravely by George Brown and divers other young gentlemen. Master MacWilliams, Bostock, with other gentlemen, were slain, with some fifty English soldiers, and as many or more hurt of the French and Walloons. So they killed and hurt some one hundred, of which were many gentlemen and officers. Some prisoners were taken on both sides. By the enemy's own confession they had slain and hurt above four hundred, whereof some were of good account.

[70] Hand-to-hand fighting by the pikemen.   [71] Enfilading fire.
[72] A corrupt form of the word "ensign." Here the standard-bearer is meant.

The surprise of Brielle in Holland by Monsieur de Lumey, Count de la Marck

At this instant Monsieur de Lumey, otherwise called the Count de la Marck, being on the coast of England with the Prince of Orange's directions, finding the seamen named before, I mean Lumbres, Bartel Entens van Mentheda, Ruychaver, and Schoonewal, they made a party betwixt them to take Brielle in Holland. True it is, the Prince of Orange had intelligence with most towns in Holland, but not with Brielle that ever I could learn. At this time there were but few Spaniards in Holland; in Brielle some hundred; in divers other places so many or fewer.

Hereupon this Count de la Marck and these captains gathered into some eight sails (the most flyboats) [73] seven hundred Walloons, Dutch, some English and Scots, all mariners. Arriving at Brielle, they landed, having drums, trumpets, and ensigns with them sufficient to have furnished thrice their numbers. At their sight the simple Spanish governor thought himself betrayed, judging that these troops would never have come hither without intelligence with the townsmen. The rest of the Spanish made proud faces, as though they meant to abide their fury and siege. Notwithstanding, they signified a fear unto the burgesses in sending their baggage and women toward Rotterdam. The Count and his captains approached with courage and withal landed three pieces out of their ships, with straw, pitch, and wood. He approached the gate and put the same soon on fire. In the meantime the Spaniards escaped toward Rotterdam.

Thus was Brielle won without blows in such sort that all Holland revolted, saving Amsterdam, but divers towns would accept no garrison. Notwithstanding, the Prince politicly wrote unto the Count to use them with all courtesy, agreeing with

[73] Originally Dutch *vlieboot*, a boat used on the *Vlie*, or channel leading out of the Zuider Zee.

their humors, suffering them to do what they listed, as well for religion as for government, whereby he gained all their hearts, for at that instant the most of the popular were papists. The Count de la Marck had almost marred all with his government, for albeit he was valiant and liberal, yet was he lascivious, willful, and obstinate, in such sort that he would enjoy any wench or woman that pleased him. Also he called an abbot and his friars into a chamber where he forced them to deny their Mass and to preach against it, in case they would not be hanged. Besides these, he committed many other disorders so as his insolency had almost thrust the Prince and his faction out of Holland.

❦

The Flushingers grow in jealousy against Tseraerts, their Governor, offering his place unto Captain Morgan, who refused it for love he bore unto Tseraerts, otherwise he had small reason in doing it

The French, Walloons, and Dutch which were in Flushing had been for the most part in the wars before, and divers of the basest sort would take anything they could carry away and lived at far greater charges to the burgesses than the English did. For indeed the English at that time were raw and looked for no more than bare victuals, lodging, and promise of pay. Hereupon the burgesses grew in great liking with our nation, insomuch that for a small suspect they would have made Captain Morgan their Governor and have cashiered Tseraerts, having no occasion but that he had a brother that dwelt amongst the enemies, whom the enemies forced to write unto the Governor to persuade him to run a course on their sides. Without doubt Tseraerts was honest unto the cause, for his brother's message and letters came no sooner unto him but he showed them unto his captains and the principal burgesses. Also this was he that commanded afterward chiefly in Haarlem. Captain Morgan, finding this man honest unto him, friended him also unto the popular, refused their offer, and maintained Tseraerts what he could in his place. Notwithstanding, few men of war would have done it unless a man had been greatly beholding unto him, I mean far more than he was to Tseraerts, considering what a rich strong government Flushing was. To say troth, this Captain had never any great ambition in him, although fortune presented fair unto him often beside this time. Also, immediately he wrote letters into England which showed the strength and goodness of the place. Withal, he procured Sir Humphrey Gilbert to come over to be colonel over the English soldiers, which he might have easily obtained himself. Hereupon Sir Humphrey contracted with the Flushingers to come unto them with 1,500 English besides those who were with them before. In the meantime the Count de la Marck assured the most part of Holland.

❧

Rotterdam surprised by the Count of Bossu, by the mere simplicity of the burgesses, where the Count showeth great cruelty upon the poor people, which was the occasion that all or the most of the towns in Holland received either garrisons or governors, principally Dort, which was resolved before to the contrary. But after this cruelty they suffered themselves easily to be surprised by the Count de la Marck

Rotterdam being without garrison, the Count Bossu approached it with some troops of Spaniards and Walloons from Utrecht. Being arrived within a quarter of a league, he placed his troops in ambush at a little castle in a small wood on the riverside toward Dort, leaving with them his lieutenant governor and giving him charge at the shooting of pieces to dislodge with all speed toward the town. The Count, being Governor of Holland and of Utrecht, came to the gates with some two hundred Walloons and Flemings and, leaving them within ten score of the port, went himself unto the port with some ten or twelve gentlemen, offering to enter. They shut the wicket against them. He showed them how he was their Governor and countryman, advised them not to deal so and to look unto themselves, else he would make them know him. Withal he desired some of the burgesses to go fetch the burgomasters unto the port that he might speak with them. In this town there was no garrison, but burgesses, poor men of war, as you may judge by their government. The burgomasters being arrived, the Count used fine speeches to persuade them to let him enter with those men, to save them from the heretics, as he termed the Prince of Orange's faction. They answered that they durst do nothing without the consent of their burgesses in general, and that they would assemble themselves presently in their townhouse and use their best means to persuade them to follow his directions, promising to return presently unto him.

Being departed, this Count, who was a good soldier and of good understanding, knew the multitude would cry against the Spanish, wherefore he thought the sooner he began his play the better. And first he did deliver some pieces of gold unto the guard, desiring them to fetch him good store of wine and beer, the which was brought presently. He and his company began to carouse, one with another, and with the guard, in such sort that they opened the little wicket to speak with the Count. Being armed under his coat and valiant, he gave signal unto his troops and therewith rushed in with some five or six gentlemen, giving blows of pistols and swords on the poor guard, in such sort that his two hundred entered and kept the port until the ambush named before entered. Then he marched unto the market place, executing all he could find in his way, thence through the town as pleased him, where he slew a great number and sacked what he listed. In this sort (God knows) he soon mastered the town. The Prince of Orange, hearing this, acquainted many of his friends with this action of Count Bossu, showing that he knew he would do the like in other places unless good guards were kept, which could never be without some garrison or at the least governors that understood the wars. In those days the names of soldiers were odious unto them. Notwithstanding, they feared the Spaniards so much that rather than to accompany with them they would accept devils. Whereupon divers agreed to accept garrisons and the most of all to receive governors, except Dort. But finally the Prince so used the matter with them that all were content that Dort should be surprised, but not with murder and sack as the Spanish did at Rotterdam. After this resolution, the Prince wrote unto the Count de la Marck and his captains to do the best they could to surprise Dort. Withal he wrote unto him both to desire and to command him to use the burgesses with all courtesy, assuring them of Holland to redress all the Count's abuses at their next meeting, which should be before long, sending them the copy of his letters to the Count. In the meantime he undertook the Count should leave his insolency and be guided by the Prince's directions.

The Count made ready a great number of *schuits*,[74] having placed some thousand soldiers among them with a great number of trumpets and ensigns, leaving Brielle, notwithstanding, in good order of defense, for his victory increased his forces. He took Strijen, right against Dort. The next morning before day he landed his men at the head before the fair, strong, and rich town of Dort, invincible without famine or treason, having

[74] Williams writes the word "skutes." A *schuit* is a boat or barge and the plural in Dutch is *schuiten*. The word is frequently found in English travel accounts.

in it a garrison and munition with a good governor. This fortunate, willful Count with his shows and looks entered the town without blows. By this time the Count's deputies had sent him three English companies under the conduct of the Captains Morris, Drise, and Reade.

᪣

The arrival of Sir Humphrey Gilbert, which was the first regiment of Englishmen that served the Netherlanders against the Spanish king, with our follies before Bruges and Sluis

Also Colonel Gilbert arrived at Flushing with ten English bands, at whose arrival Flushing was most assured. Hearing that the town of Mons was in great distress, and of the Prince of Orange's retreat, with his success, Tseraerts and Colonel Gilbert devised their best means to relieve Count Ludwig. Having a little intelligence with some burgesses of Bruges, Tseraerts and Sir Humphrey resolved to enter Flanders. And so, leaving a good garrison in Flushing, they landed at Nieuwehaven right against Flushing some fourteen hundred Englishmen, four hundred Walloons and Flemings, with some six hundred brave Frenchmen newly arrived from La Rochelle under the conduct of the Captains La Rivière, Gentane, and others. Presently we took our march toward Sluis, and being arrived at a village called Aardenburg, we resolved there to stay, both to prove if we could do any good on Sluis and to have further intelligence from Bruges. This place was a league from Sluis and three leagues from Bruges.

The next night Tseraerts and Sir Humphrey sent some eight hundred English, French, and Walloons, giving them charge to keep themselves close as near Sluis as they could until they heard further from them. Before day we placed our ambush near the ports in such sort that at the opening of the gates (had our men known the wars then as divers of them did since) we might have easily entered the town. To say troth, those that sent us were as ignorant as ourselves. In such sort that we did no more than we were commanded, which was to lie close. Notwithstanding, divers people came amongst us; some we took and some we suffered to go back again. The enemy, having discovered our numbers and lodging, sallied some two hundred shot, where we fell to hot skirmish, but all we were lodged in three places, not able to succor one another suddenly. Nevertheless half our troops, charging them resolutely, forced them to run one after another into the ports. At this alarm Tseraerts and Sir Humphrey, hearing the artillery going off, marched with the rest.

Being arrived, the Governor, like an old soldier, politicly to win time to advertise the Duke of Alva, held Sir Humphrey and Tseraerts in a parley as though he meant to deliver both town and castle unto them. Withal, he requested them to retire unto their lodgings where they were before, or else to lodge nearer where pleased them. Hereupon they retired to Aardenburg, leaving their first troops in a village hard by the town. The next day our governors were desirous to have the Captain of Sluis his resolution, who, seeing he could not defer them longer, requested them to take patience that day and the next morning he would keep promise with them. The next morning ours marched with great glory to receive the town, as we thought. Being hard by the port, the Governor welcomed us with a good volley of shot, making us to retire faster than we came by discharging their artillery against us.

Having received some loss, Tseraerts and Sir Humphrey retired into Aardenburg, to their grief. With this stratagem the Governor of Sluis won four days, in which time he advertised his general of our meaning, who sent the Count of Roeulx with certain horsemen into Bruges and a good troop of footmen marching after him. Notwithstanding, Tseraerts and Sir Humphrey dislodged with our forces and marched unto Bruges. At the break of day Sir Humphrey sent his trumpet to summon the town. The trumpeter's horse was killed with a shot from the rampire, and they made answer unto divers gentlemen who were approached near the walls that the Count de Roeulx desired all our troops to stay where we were, assuring us either within four-and-twenty hours the Count would deliver us the town or find means to hang us all, at the least our confederates in the town. Sir Humphrey was in great choler, swearing divers oaths that he would put all to the sword unless they would yield. After staying some six or eight hours, Tseraerts, understanding the wars better than Sir Humphrey, persuaded him to retire, withal assuring him unless he would do it quickly and in good order he and his troops would repent it, for the peasants advertised him there were divers troops of horsemen entered the town and a great number of footmen marched toward it, which would arrive within four hours. Being in a march, we doubled our paces in such sort that we recovered Aardenburg that night.

To say troth, the Count Roeulx was either a white-livered soldier or an ignorant captain, else he and his horsemen might have slain a great number of our men, our march was so disorderly. Insomuch as, had the Count been a brave captain, with three hundred horsemen he might have defeated our troops. After our retreat the Count executed many burgesses who had intelligence with us.

Tseraerts being arrived at Aardenburg, we resolved to remain there certain days. This place was such that it might have been kept against double our numbers. Besides, betwixt us and Flushing we had meadows and woodland countries, in such wise that horsemen could not hurt us marching in any good order. Resting in Aardenburg two days, we had intelligence that there was marching from Ghent to Bruges sixteen pieces of artillery with some munition, conducted with one of the Count's captains like himself. Whereupon Tseraerts and Sir Humphrey sent three hundred English, French, and Walloons of the best sort, giving the charge unto Rowland Yorke, lieutenant to Captain Morgan, and unto Tristan and Ambroise le Duc over the French and Walloons.

Having received direction, we marched four leagues off and placed our ambush by the break of day in the highway where the convoy was to pass. We had not stayed eight hours but we might discover the convoy, which marched as followeth: before, they had some fifty horsemen; behind as many; with a good band of footmen Walloons; the artillery and munition in the midst. At their sight, commandment was given unto us to lie very close until they were entered our ambush, which was on both sides of a great way that passed through a small grove of wood. We had gotten some twenty or thirty jades [75] or mares, which we trimmed up with old saddles, cushions, and halters that we got in boors' houses [76] as we passed. Those we placed behind the ambush, who had commandment to lie close until the ambush discharged their volley, then to charge with all resolution. These jades were in the charge of Ambroise le Duc, the Walloon, an expert soldier who had seen service on horseback often before. The convoy being entered the ambush, our volley went off in good order, in such sort that their first fifty horsemen ran on their footmen. Withal, Ambroise le Duc charged with the mares and jades. So did our footmen enter the highways against theirs in such short that their horsemen ran away, leaving their footmen and convoy to be executed by us, which were for the most part with small loss or none at all to ourselves.

Out of this place we arrived at Aardenburg the next day, with all the artillery and munition in like order as we found them. By a bridge we stayed and took a great number of boats laden with woolsacks and merchandise which we returned all into our quarter.

To say troth, these three leaders named before were the min-

---

[75] "Jades" means "mares."   [76] Farmhouses.

ions[77] at all attempts of our troops in those days. The next day after our arrival at Aardenburg, intelligence was brought that Mons was delivered and Malines taken and sacked, and that Julián Romero was marching into Flanders to assist the Count of Roeulx with twenty ensigns of footmen and some cornets of horsemen. This news made us not to take counsel twice for our retreat, whereupon we marched with all speed toward Flushing.

℘

Our first offer to assiege Goes, with our sudden retreat

Being arrived right against Flushing at Nieuwehaven, we made stand where Tseraerts and Sir Humphrey took resolution to assiege Goes, which stands in an island of Zeeland, bordering on Brabant and Flanders. Our shipping being arrived from Flushing, we embarked and arrived the next day at night by Baarland, a village of the said island. After anchoring and giving directions, Rowland Yorke, Vitran, and Ambroise le Duc landed with their accustomed troops or more, albeit divers were slain at the exploit of Sluis and the convoy. The bravest youths desired to go always with the first, in such sort that these were always well accompanied. Being landed upon the ditch which environs the island, the enemy, perceiving (as it is like) our navy long before we anchored, sallied the most of the soldiers out of the town and placed themselves in ambush in a village hard by the place we landed at through which we must pass to go to the town. After Tseraerts and Sir Humphrey were landed, the vanguard was given to Captain Morgan and commandment to Yorke, Vitran, and Ambroise le Duc to enter the village.

The enemies having with them their governor, a brave captain named Pedro Pacheco,[78] kept themselves close in the vil-

---

[77] Persons specially favored.
[78] The Governor of Goes was Isidoro Pacheco.

lage until Yorke and we entered the ambush. Then they delivered a hot volley of shot upon us and withal charged with some hundred pikes, in such sort that with much ado the one half of our troops could recover the place where Captain Morgan stood with our seconds.[79] True it is, the enemy stood in the village round about the way where we marched and received us at the entry of some hundred of ours into the village out of the narrow way, where we passed and could not march above five in a rank, wherefore they found us good cheap. Our retreat was so fast that the enemy followed us upon the heels into the troops which Captain Morgan led, who charged them resolutely with his armed men in such sort that the enemies ran back. But wisely he had placed half his men in the village for his retreat, who delivered their volley on Captain Morgan in such sort that he stayed for Tseraerts and Sir Humphrey, who were not within a mile by reason they stood at the first alarm, and not without marvel, for I persuade myself the most of them were afraid.

I am to blame to judge their minds, but let me speak troth. I do assure you it was not without reason, for the most of us who entered with Yorke were slain; such as escaped swam and struggled through muddy ditches. Amongst other gentlemen, Edward Argoll was slain by Sir Humphrey his standard. The enemy recovered their town, and all our troops entered Baarland some two hours after their retreat.

The next morning we dislodged toward Goes. Our vanguard being arrived within half a mile of the town, we made a stand until the rest arrived. In the meantime the enemies sallied and gave furiously into our guards, forced our first guards to run amongst our battles [80] of pikes, which stood in a large place by the house of the Count Egmond, having a bridge betwixt them and the enemy.

Notwithstanding, Captain Morgan with his brave shot entered an orchard and flanked the enemy, which stood on the

[79] Reserves.   [80] Formations of pikemen.

high ditch beating on our pikes with volleys of shot. Withal, Sir Humphrey and his armed men passed the bridge and charged the enemy with great resolution, in such sort that the enemy fell to running. Notwithstanding, our men executed a great number and amongst others three Spanish captains with divers other officers. We lost also divers of our men. You must think that in those days few of us or of the enemy knew the wars so well as since, for this Pacheco and his men quitted Zierikzee some seven days before as a place not guardable. Also, being governor of a town, he was to blame to sally with his garrison so far as Baarland, especially himself, for without doubt had Tseraerts and Sir Humphrey known of his being there with most of his troops and therewith given a right direction, it had cost him his town besides his defeat. Sir Humphrey should have directed at least half his troops to cut betwixt them and the town at the first alarm. Some may say perhaps there were no ways or he knew of none. There were other ways, although not so near. Besides, a commander that enters the enemy's countries ought to know the places that he doth attempt; if not, he ought to be furnished with guides, especially in coming to besiege a town. But we were so ignorant that we knew not our own estate, much less the enemy's. For the next day after our arrival and skirmish we marched to embark our troops, alleging we wanted artillery and munition, with all other necessaries that belonged to a siege. Before our embarking, the old soldiers Captain Gentane and Henri the Frenchman used a fine stratagem. They requested Tseraerts and Sir Humphrey to cause all their ensigns to embark with the baggage and a good number of soldiers, and to leave in a church and in a churchyard and in a great close adjoining the most of their ablest men, and they to keep close that day to see if the enemy would sally to cut off their rear guard and stragglers.

As they directed, Tseraerts and Sir Humphrey placed 1,200 of their best men in that place, which was halfways betwixt our quarter and the embarking place about a great league from the town. Our ensigns were not all aboard, but Pacheco sallied with the most of his garrison, which might be some four hundred. Being approached our first ambush, who were Walloons, a foolish officer contrary to direction discharged a volley of shot on the enemies who were some quarter of a mile before their troops, whereby all was marred. Belike our armed men gave them such sound blows in the last re-encounter that they desired no more. So upon this volley the enemy retired into their town and we embarked presently, not unwilling, for anything I could perceive. To say troth, our losses might be in a manner compared equal, from our landing to our embarking. Let me not wrong our governors too much. They said they were advertised that Goes was void of garrison saving some hundred and that they knew nothing of Pacheco's arrival. Being embarked, we arrived at our town of Flushing, where we landed under our town and marched to a village named Zoutelande three leagues from Flushing in the same island. Before this time Veere revolted also unto the Prince of Orange by reason of their governor, Monsieur de Rollé.

꿍

The camisado given our troops, being lodged in Zoute-lande, by Monsieur de Beauvoir and Don Ruffello, where our men defended themselves and overthrew the enemy most valiantly, with our second siege of Goes, where we were defeated shamefully by the negligence and ignorance of our governor

Monsieur de Beauvoir, Governor of Middelburg, and Don Ruffello, hearing of our arrival in Zoutelande (belike Pacheco advertised them that we had received greater loss than we did before Goes), thinking our courage qualified, prepared all their forces to defeat us with a camisado. To do it the more terribly they prepared a great number of halters, giving them to their soldiers with a commandment to hang all the prisoners they should take. The old saying is true: it is no surety to reckon without an host. Being ready after directions given, they sallied out of Middelburg some two thousand Spaniards and Walloons at the shutting of their gates and took the next way toward the sandy hills betwixt Flushing and Zoutelande. As God would, certain of the victualers, discovering their march, cut their mares out of their wagons, by which means they recovered Zoutelande an hour before the enemy arrived, which, next unto the Almighty's will, saved all our troops. Having the alarm, the enemy's vanguard was in sight, which presently chargeth our guards, making them to run into the camp and to quit the sandy hills. All their forces seconded with all speed very resolutely, forcing our first and second troops to run into our place of arms, which was near unto the other side of the town in a churchyard and a large street before it, so as they won our artillery, turning the same toward us. But resolutely our officers gathered a sufficient number of armed men into the market place, who, being led valiantly with brave captains, charged the enemy, giving them a retreat and defeat beyond our fieldpieces. Here they came again with a fresh charge, but our armed men re-encountered them at the push of pike most valiantly, in such sort that the ensign-bearers, Philip Watkins, Thomas Lovell, John Hamon, with divers others, brake their ensign-staves at the push of pike. So our men gave the enemy a full overthrow, driving them clean out of the camp and following them in defeat halfway to Middelburg. After, our men hung a number of them with their own halters.

This piece of service was one of the best and worthiest encounters that our men had from that time to this hour in all their wars of the Low Countries. The enemies were all overthrown. Notwithstanding, many escaped by reason of the ditches and narrow ways, especially the most of their officers and leaders, by reason of their horses and jades. Ours scaped not scot-free, for we had slain and hurt about 250, many of them officers, and amongst others the Captains Bouser, Bedes, and Bostock, English; besides Walloons and French which served most valiantly. But the chief praise next unto God ought to be given to the English ensigns [81] and armed men. Captain Walter Morgan served very well, who was overthrown with a musket shot in the head of the armed men.[82] All the rest did most valiantly. Some will blame me for the naming of our own losses, but it is a shame for a soldier to write less than truth. There can be no brave encounter without men slain on both sides. True it is, the fewer, the better conduct; but the more dies, the more honor to the fight.

This encounter so encouraged our men that Tseraerts and Sir Humphrey resolved to return to Goes. After finishing their preparations and orders, we landed at the same village we did before, in number above three thousand English, French, and Walloons, for our troops were increased with Rollé and his garrison of Veere. Our second landing was in better order than the first by reason our ships attempted the island in two places, but all or the most part that carried soldiers were at the landing place. The other, being so many vessels in number, approached the shore in such sort that the enemy durst not separate their forces to attempt both, fearing that the other would cut betwixt them and the town. Being all on the shore, we marched unto a fair village named Biezelinge some league from Goes, where we lodged that night and the next day.

The second night at midnight we marched toward Goes; before six of the clock in the morning we were all within an English mile of the town. Finding the inconvenience of our

---

[81] The meaning here may be either the English companies or the English officers, probably the former.

[82] I.e., at the head of the armed men.

last skirmish in the one place, order was given to the companies of the Captains Morgan, Henri, Bernaert, and Vitran to march with all speed to attempt the fort which stood on the head of the haven which entered into Goes; and if the enemy would not quit their fort, then to lodge on the one ditch betwixt them and the town, where they stood in battle on the other ditch to see the effect of our attempting the fort.

Being hot in skirmish with the fort, according to our direction, a company of our men began to seek means to pass over the ditches to cut betwixt the fort and the town. There was also a way that passed through the meadows from the ditch where our battle stood, whither Sir Humphrey and Tseraerts sent many to second us. The enemy, perceiving our resolution to lodge betwixt the fort and the town, quitted the fort. Notwithstanding, Yorke with most of C. Morgan's [83] company re-encountered them on the ditch in such sort that half of those who were in the fort were cut off before they could recover the town. True it is, the enemy had reason to quit the fort by reason they were not victualed but from hand to mouth; neither was it worthy of any great munition, because it could not endure any battery.

Being entered the suburbs, Pacheco sallied with great courage and skirmished in such sort that our first troops were forced to stand for their fellows, at which instant the enemy fired all or the most of the salthouses. Our men being arrived close together, we charged Pacheco, forced their troops to double their paces into their gates, and withal lodged and placed our first guards at a chapel within eight score of the town, where we stayed and made good until all our troops were lodged. By reason of our small army we could not assure the one half of the town, for the garrison were eight hundred strong, all natural Spaniards commanded by more expert leaders than ourselves. Yet having made our trenches and approaches, we landed six

[83] Captain Morgan's company.

pieces of battery within six score of the walls, which did beat on the port toward the haven. Perceiving those pieces could not make any breach to content our governors, we dislodged them to beat on the bulwarks which flanked that curtain. Having battered this parapet and made it fit, as we thought, to be attempted with a small scalado, resolution was taken to assault it the next night.

In the meantime so great a pick and jealousy grew betwixt Sir Humphrey and Tseraerts that each would fain disgrace his fellow. Notwithstanding, both agreed to attempt the scalado. After midnight we dislodged from our quarter some two thousand of our best men, all in camisados,[84] with scaling ladders, God knows like ignorant soldiers, else we would never have attempted a scalado on such a troop, for lightly a scalado never takes place unless it be on a simple troop or a negligent guard having a rampire or fort to defend. Notwithstanding, ambition and courage so pushed us on that Sir Humphrey and Tseraerts, being approached, advanced up their ladders; so did a great number of gentlemen and soldiers on sundry ladders. The enemy politicly kept close until many were ready to enter; then they discharged a volley of shot full in our faces, killing many, and withal their armed men advanced to the push of the pike in such sort that they dismounted the most without ladders. At which terror we retired without commandment until we came under the dike where the enemy's shot could not hurt us, and not without reason, for, being on the bulwark, it was flanked from the curtain in such sort that none could abide it. Neither could we join with the enemy unless he listed, by reason of a dike betwixt both on which they had a drawbridge at their commandment.

At this scalado Sir Humphrey and Tseraerts served very valiantly; he that escaped best of both had sundry hagabusha-

[84] Williams means the men were wearing white shirts in preparation for the camisado.

77

does [85] on their armors and camisados, I mean their shirts that covered their armors. Many young gentlemen and officers performed also courageous service. Divers were slain and hurt, among others one Bourege was taken by the enemy, whom they commended greatly for his valor, but he died afterwards of his hurts in their hands.

This attempt so quailed our courage that we despaired of the town. Notwithstanding, resolution was taken to continue the siege until the Prince of Orange were advertised how the world went. Hereupon Tseraerts, Sir Humphrey, and Rowland [Yorke] dispatched posts to the Prince, both to advertise him and to procure more means. The Prince, understanding our case, dispatched letters to the towns of Holland and to the Count de la Marck to desire them to do their best endeavor to assist us before Goes. The Count sent his lieutenant, Bartel Entens van Mentheda, with some two thousand Netherlanders and Almains. Being joined with us, they gave some courage at the first; but when their discipline and valor was tried we found them simpler men than ourselves, yea, so raw that they brought us every day into more disorders. Nevertheless, the sight of our numbers caused us to besiege the town round about. Belike the enemy feared us or wanted some necessaries and, finding means to acquaint the Duke of Alva with their wants, he sent with all speed his Colonel Mondragón with his regiment of Walloons and about seven companies more of Walloons and Spaniards, who might be in all some three thousand strong.

This colonel was expert, valiant, and vigilant. Being arrived at Bergen-op-Zoom and finding our forces masters of the seas and making good guard round about the island where we were, he was in great pain and knew not how to pass the water. By good espials and guides he found the island easy to be entered at a low water from the bank of Brabant, where the passage in the deepest place was not above four foot and for more than

[85] Harquebus shots.

half the way dry sands; but at quarter-flood all was covered
with seas at the least six English miles, so as his troops must
recover the dike of the island from the place where they entered in less than three hours or else be overflown with the sea.
Also, being ready to enter on our dike, had our governor kept
good guards with any valor, his troops must needs have been
defeated. Also, he could not bring many hands to fight in order,
the narrowness of the place where he marched was such; but
this colonel, remembering the strait commandment of his general, fearing the town to be in greater wants than indeed it
was, resolved to pass and landed without resistance. Notwithstanding, he lost in his passage near two hundred. Besides, he
and his troops were so wet and weary that they remained all
that night in the place where they landed, which was about two
great leagues from our camp. Then judge you what would have
become of his troops had we been commanded by expert governors and charged them at their landing with half our numbers. In reason, we had defeated them.

The next morning Mondragón took his march toward Goes,
having intelligence with the town, and being in sight, the town
sallied [86] and entered into hot skirmish with our guards on the
side from their succors in such sort that the most of our camp
made head toward them. While we were in hot skirmish with the
garrison, Mondragón passed his men through the town pell-mell
with ours in such sort that they forced our guards to run and
quit all our trenches, even to the fort at the head of the water
toward the sea. This fort was so little that it could not hold three
hundred of our men, wherefore our disorder was great in seeking means to escape into our navy, which anchored within an
harquebus shot of the fort. A great number were drowned besides those that were slain, and some yielded unto the enemy,
especially those who were in the fort. Divers officers were carried prisoners into the castle of Antwerp and amongst others

[86] The troops in the town sallied.

79

Captains Tristan and Vitran. Thus ended our ignorant poor siege, and but for the *schuits* and small boats which came hard by the shore to receive us in, all had been lost.

Our blow was so great that Sir Humphrey and the most of our men, not being acquainted with such disasters, sought all means to return into England. Notwithstanding, before we embarked, Sir William Morgan arrived from the Prince with authority from the Prince and the States in Holland to make large offers to stay Sir Humphrey and his regiment for their service, but all would not serve to stay either Sir Humphrey or any of his troops. Whilst our siege of Goes endured, Worst, the admiral, and his seamen won Zierikzee without blows. By that you may perceive that Pacheco and his were not exceeding expert in quitting such a place in such manner as they did.

I did hear also that Sir William Pelham was sent from England to view the seat of Flushing. Being returned, they said his report was that it was a place not worthy to be kept, meaning not sufficient to withstand so great an enemy any long time. If that be true, we were not very great captains at that time, for then without fellow he was accounted our chiefest soldier. By this time the Prince had gotten a sure footing in Holland, so as all places of any importance were his.

&

The Duke of Alva assieges Haarlem, where many disasters fell on both sides, which siege may be called the tedi-ousest, dearest, and painfulest of any in those days

The Duke of Alva, seeing the people generally ready to revolt with the least show the Prince could make, resolved to gather his forces and to charge the Hollanders with all fury, swearing to his captains and soldiers that the spoil of Holland should be theirs upon condition they would execute all they found. Having prepared a mighty army with all necessaries, he dislodged out of Brussels toward Holland. Being arrived at Nijmegen, he passed the rivers of Waal and Rhine in the dead of winter and against all reason marched from Arnhem toward Utrecht. His high marshal or master of his camp general was Chiappino Vitelli; Don Juan de Mendoza was general of his horsemen; his general of the artillery, Monsieur de Cressonière; his *maestres de campo* were Juan Bautista del Monte, Dorkus, Julián Romero, Juan Francisco de Valdéz, Sancho de Avila, and Mondragón. There were with him also many others of nobility and gentlemen of quality, as well Italians, Almains, Burgundians, and Netherlanders as also of Spanish.

Being arrived at Amsterdam, he commanded his son Don Fadrique, Chiappino Vitelli, and Mendoza to march with the vanguard and to engage the town of Haarlem in such sort that nothing could pass from it to Leiden or to any other place by land. Having placed four regiments of Almains and Walloons well entrenched in the wood hard by the town and in the ways toward Leiden, Don Fadrique placed himself with a Spanish tercio or regiment well entrenched in a village and a strong house between the town and the sea, and so lodged the rest of his companies that the town sallies were cut off, saving on the one quarter, which was meadows and marsh, toward the Meer.[87] In the town were the most of the Prince's best captains, namely Monsieur Tseraerts, Steven, Buts, Balfour, Smith, with divers others of the Scots, French, Almains, and Walloons, amongst whom were some two hundred English in sundry companies without any ensign of their own. The garrison in the whole might be some three thousand soldiers. They caused also about six hundred burgesses to carry arms, besides two thousand and more of all sorts of people sufficient to supply the place of pioneers, of which were some three hundred women all under one ensign. The women's captain was a most stout dame named Captain Margaret Kenau.

Having divided the town into quarters, and giving charge of

[87] Haarlemmermeer is meant.

every quarter unto a principal chief, they fell to working in great numbers on the weakest parts of the city and mended continually some part of the fortifications, in such sort that within one month their town was three times stronger than the first hour the enemy encamped before it. They kept also two small sconces [88] on the mouth of the water that ran from the town into the Meer, which assured the passage that ways, by which means they received daily all manner of commodities that pleased the Prince and the States of Holland to send them.

The Prince kept at Delft in Holland. He chose for his lieutenant of the wars the Baron of Batenburg; for general of his horsemen and marshal Monsieur de Carloo; for admiral of the Meer for that service one Marinus Brandt. By reason of the Spanish long delays in their resolutions about their martial affairs, the Prince dispatched away his chiefs with some five thousand soldiers and about sixty hoys and cromsters, of which six were galiots and frigates.[89] This army arrived at the Kaag within three leagues of Haarlem, a place environed with waters, where because the Spanish could not attempt by reason the Prince was master upon the waters, the Baron Batenburg furnished Haarlem at his pleasure with all necessaries. There stood in the main right against it on the Meer side a village named Sassenheim, where he landed and entrenched very strongly. In that place he encamped with some six hundred horsemen and the most of his footmen. At the Kaag there was no danger, wherefore he anchored his shipping hard by the shore, leaving for their guard six hundred soldiers with the admiral and one Hasselaar.

By this time the Duke of Alva arrived before the town with his whole forces, artillery, and munition, amounting in the whole near to thirty thousand, of which might be some thou-

---

[88] Blockhouses or strong points.

[89] *Hoy,* a small vessel usually rigged as a sloop; *cromster* or *crumster,* also a small vessel, a variety of hoy or galley; *galiot* here probably means a Dutch *galjoot,* a fishing vessel or small cargo boat; *frigate* means here a light, swift vessel which could be rowed if necessary.

sand and five hundred horsemen. He needed no great cavalry, by reason he was assured there would be but few against him. Also those grounds did not serve for great troops of horsemen to fight in. After viewing the strong seat of the Baron of Batenburg and perceiving no good could be done upon his troops to affront him, he advanced Juan Bautista del Monte with five cornets [of] Italians, who entrenched strongly with sixteen companies of footmen in a village called Hillegom half the way betwixt both our companies. Afterwards he began to make his approaches carefully, sparing neither pioneers nor cost, to spare his soldiers. Before he planted his battery the town made many brave sallies, killed a great number with small loss to themselves. Once they carried divers ensigns out of their enemy's trenches and nailed sundry pieces of battery.[90] After placing his battery and playing furiously, he gave two sharp assaults, which were defended worthily by the besieged to the enemy's great loss, of whom a great number of quality were slain and hurt, and amongst others the brave master of the camp, Julián Romero, lost his eye with a harquebusado. The enemy often possessed the breach, but being entered their half-moon, I mean the trench which the defendants made overthwart the breach within, they were murdered like dogs. The defendants had divers fowlers [91] and other pieces loaden with nails and small shot which they placed on the corners of their half-moon. Those were discharged full against the enemies, being entered upon the breach. Also they had placed a great number of small shot in houses both high and low, full of cannoneers who flanked the half-moon, and besides the half-moon was double manned with musketeers and calivers.[92] The Duke of Alva his losses were so great that, perceiving the brave resolution of the defendants, he gave over his assaults and began to mine and to approach carefully with sap and other stratagems. Sometimes he would mount

[90] I.e., spiked the guns.   [91] Light cannon.
[92] Calivers were light muskets, hence troops armed with light muskets.

cages on masts made with planks and such devices of musket-proof. In those he would place divers musketeers, who by reason of their height did beat into the trenches of the half-moon. The defendants, good cannoneers, plagued those cages in such sort that often the cages, birds and all, fell down and brake their necks in their own trenches; so at last no birds could be found to sing in cages where firework and cannon shot could annoy them.

His mines took little effect. Some the defendants found with countermine. One mine being passed under a bulwark before it was found, and then discovered, the defendants made such trenches round about it that, the mine being fired and the enemies entered, the trench plagued them like the half-moon, so as they were driven to quit their mine as before they had done their breach. Another time they battered a new bulwark, and the defendants perceiving they would lodge in it, left rampiring against their battery [93] and fell to mining their own bulwark. After making many trenches round about it and placing divers barrels of powder in their mine, the enemies offered to enter. The defendants quitted the bulwark, suffered the enemies to enter in great numbers, and being at the push of pike at a barrier of their trench, they fired the mine, blew, slew, and took at least 1,600, and withal sallied into their trenches and recovered their own ground where their bulwark stood, which they entrenched and kept.

The Duke of Alva his losses were so great that albeit his choler increased yet the courage of his soldiers much quailed, so that the wisest sort requested him to save his men from such furious terrors and rather to spend a long time either to famish the town or to procure the Prince's forces to fight, which he could not do without means to fight by water. Being in Amsterdam, with the resolution of his admiral, Count Bossu, and good intelligence with the principal burgesses of the said town, he

[93] Ceased repairing their ramparts.

resolved to cut a passage from the Southern Sea [94] into the Haarlemmermeer, which they did and passed some forty-five sails, whereof most were greater than those of the Prince's. These they armed and double manned with the best sort of soldiers out of their camp, besides their mariners. Anchoring close under a fort of theirs, not far from ours, they resolved to besiege the two forts at the mouth of the water that came from the town to the Meer. Having those, they were sure to stop that passage and to famish the town without giving battle. In short time they made a platform to beat these forts, which would hold good if their shipping could stay where they were.

The Prince, hearing their intent, commanded the Baron of Batenburg to prepare all his navy to attempt the Spanish fleet. By this time Colonel Morgan was arrived with ten English companies, who by reason he was but newly landed stood on some points of contract with the Prince. But the service required haste, and the Prince commanded the Baron of Batenburg to advance his navy with all speed and to use all diligence to succor the distressed sconces. And albeit the English regiment stood on terms, Colonel Morgan (his own band, commanded by Rowland Yorke, being arrived some month before their fellows) offered himself, and so did his lieutenant, Captain Bingham, with divers others, to serve where the Prince would command them. But their regiment refused to march without money. To say troth, they were promised to be mustered and paid at their landing.

The Baron of Batenburg, wanting soldiers to man both his navy and his trenches at Sassenheim, was forced to depart with the navy before toward Haarlem, God knoweth nothing well manned in respect of the Spanish. The Spanish admiral, having intelligence, was ready with his navy double manned, wanting no necessaries, for the fair and rich town of Amsterdam had furnished them with all wants, especially with store of mariners.

[94] Zuider Zee.

Being approached within sight one of another, we found the Spanish in good order of battle, keeping close together. They advanced toward us, triumphing with drums, trumpets, and glistering armors with great courage, so as the sight quailed the courage of our white-livered general and cowardly admiral; in such sort that, being approached near ready to board each other, our general and our admiral shrank out of our first rank backwards; and, advancing their fellows forwards, both themselves and divers others of our best vessels made all the sails they could to fly, leaving their poor companies engaged to the mercy of their enemies, by whom (God knows) they were soon discountenanced. Our admiral and general with our best sails escaped to the Kaag, as I said before, a place of ours where we kept garrison; the rest of our navy made to the contrary shore from Haarlem. Divers escaped by reason they drew far lesser water than the Spanish; divers were boarded and burned, among others two hoys where Yorke and Captain Morgan's company was. Notwithstanding, half our men escaped with leaping into the water and recovered the shore.

Thus lost we our sea battle, principally for want of soldiers to man thoroughly our ships, but partly with ill directions and cowardly executions of the Baron of Batenburg and Admiral Marinus Brandt; for no general or chief can excuse himself escaping out of an overthrow without staying with the last troops that fight. After this our two sconces were lost and Haarlem engaged to be lost without succors by land, which could not be without battle. Shortly after, the town began to fall to distresses, having in it at the least 1,600 mouths, with no means to be rid of any of them but through the enemy's camp, which they offered to pass often, but always they were returned into the town or massacred in the camp. The poor Prince, perceiving the distress of the town, sought all means to relieve it. Having no other means, he went to public banquets where he encouraged the Hollanders to take arms and adventure themselves with his men of war rather than suffer their distressed countrymen to perish. These poor Hollanders, having engaged themselves with promise, resolved to meet on a day in the camp of Sassenheim. Being arrived, the Baron of Batenburg and Monsieur de Carloo, general of his horsemen, took resolution to try the fortune of wars with the enemy rather than to suffer the world to cry out that the town was lost without blows on their sides; and, thinking his name to be infamous (as indeed it was) for the sea fight, he thought it better to be buried dead than alive. Hereupon he dislodged from his trenches of Sassenheim, accompanied with some six thousand footmen and six hundred horsemen and having with him some thousand mares, upon most of the which he placed two shot apiece. The rest were led with boors,[95] loaded with powder and other necessaries which the town wanted greatly. Resolving to put those necessaries into the town, he advanced his forces. Being arrived hard by Hillegom, a place (as I said before) which the enemy kept, at the break of day, the enemy taking the alarm, the Baron made a stand. After conferring with his captains, he took resolution to defer their design and returned with our camp to Sassenheim.

The besieged, being in great distress for victuals, especially for munition, and finding the ill conduct of our general and chiefs, dispatched out of town their captain, Monsieur de Tseraerts, and Haultain, his lieutenant, who passed with great danger and were forced to swim many ditches hard by the enemy's guards. Being arrived at Sassenheim, bearing with them the town's resolution, which was at the first sight of our camp to sally on the enemy's trenches and so either to receive their wants into the town or to escape how they could, Tseraerts, having conferred with the Prince and the Baron at Leiden, returned to Sassenheim, where they took a full resolution either to die or succor the town. Hereupon they dislodged from Sassenheim with our army named before, having with them some six

[95] Farmers, countrymen.

hundred wagons loaded with victuals and munition, with sconces made of boards of the proof of muskets which ran on wheels, having in them places to play with sundry fieldpieces, which sconces were to join and to open as pleased our engineer every five and ten paces. Being all joined together, I mean in one, it might cover at the least three hundred men. This sconce was to be drawn with horses on both sides and in the midst until we were engaged with the enemy's small shot, then to be pushed with poles by the force of men.

Being parted with all necessaries and arrived betwixt their camp at Hillegom and the sea, the enemies took the alarm in all their quarters. Arriving within sight of their camp, they kept their men very close within their trenches and on the side of the wood, so that we could not see them. Our men within the town had made a great sally through the curtain, in such sort that they might issue out where there was neither guard nor trench of the enemy, but a traitor, leaping over the walls in the night, discovered all their intent. Whereupon the enemy prepared great quantities of straw which, being made wet, they set on fire in sundry places at such time as their couriers gave the alarm of the approach of our army when the townsmen were ready to sally out, by which means the townsmen could neither see the approaching of our army nor knew what time they ought to sally. So the enemy directed five thousand of his best footmen and three hundred horsemen to charge the townsmen if they sallied and the rest to charge our camp, if it were possible, unknown to the townsmen; and so they did by their government and fine stratagem, for at the sight of our army (being within two musket shot of their trenches) the Duke of Alva caused the five thousand footmen and three hundred horsemen to discover themselves before the breach which our men had made in the curtain. Withal he commanded the brave Baron Chevraux and Juan Bautista del Monte (who had quitted Hillegom with all his horsemen and was newly arrived in their

camp) with others to march on the sea sands until his artillery
went off in volleys, then to cut into the highways betwixt Haarlem and our camp at Sassenheim, having with them some five
hundred horsemen and about five thousand footmen. Also he
commanded his master of the camp, Julián Romero, Juan Bautista del Monte, Donkus, the Barons of Licques and of Capres,
of Fronsberg and Polwiller, to leap over the trenches with
their regiments and charge our army at the discharging of his
artillery. Also Don Juan de Mendoza, a general of his horsemen, who was hidden, as I said before, was commanded to
charge our horsemen at the going off of the artillery. The Duke
with the rest of his army stood in battle within the trenches.

Our general and chiefs placed our wagons to frontier [96] the
fairest places where their horsemen could charge us. Our Walloons, Dutch, and Flemish stood within the wagons in good
order of battle, all in one squadron with our horsemen on both
the sides toward the enemies. Our English, French, and Scots
stood some twenty score before the front of our battle.[97] As we
were busy in placing our engines, I mean our sconces and wagons, their artillery went off, and withal the enemies presented
in all quarters as they were directed. At this sight (God knows)
our courage much abated. Notwithstanding, the Baron of Batenburg and Monsieur de Carloo charged Mendoza, he having better than eight hundred horsemen and ours not six hundred, at
which charge Monsieur de Carloo, general of our horsemen, was
slain with many others of our best men. At that instant the
Baron Chevraux and Juan Bautista came on the spur toward
the Baron of Batenburg, leaving their footmen marching with
all speed on the side of ours. Upon their approach the Baron
and our horsemen ran into our wagons with all the enemy's
horsemen in their tails. Then Julián [Romero] and the rest
named before drove in the English and French shot, winning
our sconces and wagons, and our battle broke and ran toward

[96] To protect.   [97] Main body of troops.

the Meer. By reason of meadows and ditches, divers escaped into our navy, which anchored not far off under a strong sconce whose boats rowing from our ships saved many. But the Baron, our general, was slain after he had recovered our battle with the most part of our men. All or the most part of our cornets, ensigns, artillery, munition, wagons, engines, and baggage were lost.

Thus were we overthrown with ill directions and ignorant government. What prince or estate would direct their men of war, especially being more than half their own countrymen, to attempt above 26,000 good soldiers, well entrenched, governed with great captains, not being in the whole 6,500 footmen and, of those, half poor-spirited burgesses? Or what general or captain would undertake it unless he were ignorant and without judgment in martial affairs? Some will say, had our friends perished in the town without blows it had been our shame. I do confess it, having any reason to fight, but, being sure to perish both, it was our greatest shame to attempt it. If we had kept ourselves undefeated and given order to the town to have compounded with the enemy, their composition had been the better; but, being defeated, the townsmen were fain to yield to the mercy of the Duke of Alva, for the sight of our ensigns and cornets so quailed their courage that, having no other remedy, they yielded to his mercy within four days after our overthrow. But he executed the most part of them most cruelly, saving the Almains of Steinbach's regiment, who compounded for the most part to serve the King, and Balfour with a few Scottish men, who to escape the Duke of Alva's cruelty promised to kill the Prince of Orange, but, being arrived with the Prince, he confessed his promise and served him faithfully long after.

❧

The Spanish Mutinies

The Spanish mutinies; Monsieur de Hierges repulseth them at their scalado on Utrecht. The Duke of Alva assiegeth Alkmaar, where he receiveth the greatest disgrace that ever he did since he carried arms

The Duke of Alva, having won Haarlem and as he thought broken the courage of the Hollanders, thinking the Prince of Orange and them not able to furnish any place like unto Haarlem and that his cruelty on that town would terrify any garrison from hazarding themselves to be besieged, he resolved with his council of war to attempt one of the other strongest towns, as Alkmaar or Leiden, which being won, the rest or most of the others would yield. To that end he dispatched his son, Don Fadrique, accompanied with the master of his camp, General Chiappino Vitelli, giving them half his army and charge with all diligence to enclose the strong town of Alkmaar situated in North Holland; himself, with the rest of his army, officers, nobility, artillery, munition, with all other necessaries, was to second them with all speed.

His orders being set down and his army dislodged, having passed their fort of Spaarndam, the Spanish tercios began to mutiny, partly discontented for want of pay but chiefly fearing to be troubled with a more miserable lodging than they had before Haarlem. This proceeded chiefly from a few of the Netherlanders which served amongst their bands and knew the seat of Alkmaar to be an ill-favored marsh far more unwholesome than Haarlem, and knew it also to be a seat thrice stronger than Haarlem. To say troth, if it were lawful for men of war to find fault with any enterprise that their general undertakes, they had reason to fear Alkmaar, considering how their misery endured before Haarlem above ten months, in the which time they lost above twenty thousand lives, the most with sickness and misery.

Whereupon being past the fort of Spaarndam and lodged on the firm land, having neither river nor marsh betwixt them and the fair town of Utrecht, the Spanish tercios chose and forced one to be their chief, named in their language an *electo*, who is lightly one of the finest stirring spirits amongst them, well known to be stout and valiant. Sometimes they forced a person to be their *electo* against his will; but, whether he be willing or not, they will be sure to give him a strong guard of the chiefest mutineers, with such articles as if they find him faulty in the least point they will murder him had he a hundred lives. Especially he must neither sign nor write anything but in public places before them all. Likewise he must neither receive writings nor speeches but in open audience, nor do anything without their general consent. Observing their articles and orders, the multitude will respect and obey him during his government in as ample sort as the King's lieutenant, and all are sworn not to do anything without his consent; and with their general and officers they promise to free him from all matters that can be laid unto his charge, which they have observed firmly at sundry times, as I will show hereafter. And to say troth, if there can be any good orders in mutinies, the Spanish do theirs in good order and keep as good and as strait discipline during the time of their *electo* as when their officers are amongst them. As I said in my little discourse of the Spanish discipline, there can be no dangerous mutiny without a chief, which must be authorized by a prince or estate. If any of them mutineth, there must be present means to cut them off, as Alexander did his Parmenio,[98] or some other means to be assured of their persons, else ambitious chiefs will often employ armies against their own states and masters and will not fail to use their means and credits to deceive the multitude to serve their own turns. Being

[98] Parmenio or Parmenion, ca. 400–330 B.C., Macedonian, the leading general and counselor of both Philip II and Alexander. He was assassinated by order of Alexander for his part in a revolutionary plot in 330 B.C.

stirred in arms, by all reason they are irreconcilable to their princes or estates. The multitude and followers may be pardoned and forgiven, but in no reason their principal instruments can look for any sure reconcilement. But a popular multitude, either in arms or otherwise mutinied, may be appeased and reconciled easily in respect of the others, having no other instruments than were made by themselves, especially forced *electos* like unto the Spanish.

As I said before, the Spanish tercios and some six regiments of Walloons resolved to enter the city of Utrecht and to sack it rather than to miss their due pay. Whereupon they marched with all speed toward Utrecht, and in their way they carried with them all the ladders they could find in villages and churches which they thought would serve their turns. Being approached hard by the town, they found the walls well manned and in good order by reason Monsieur de Hierges, Governor of Gelderland and of Utrecht, was arrived there upon intelligence of their determinations, who commanded the captain of the castle upon his allegiance to the King to use all endeavors for the defense of the town. The castellan assured him of his loyalty to the uttermost of his power.

To be the better assured of his Spanish garrison, Monsieur de Hierges caused half the garrison of the castle to sally and to man the curtain where the mutineers attempted. Before they offered any attempt, Hierges sent a Spanish drum unto them, assuring them, rather than they should enter the town, he and as many as loved the King's service would die in the place. Notwithstanding, the mutineers resolved and advanced the scale,[99] giving their fury on the curtain next unto the citadel, thinking belike that their fellows within would not be cruel against them. But, being in the ditch and having placed their ladders to the rampire, both Hierges and the captain of the castle and all the rest plagued them with volleys of shot both great and small in

[99] I.e., continued their plan to scale the walls.

such sort that happy was he that could return first, leaving behind them all or the most part of their ladders with many of their men slain or hurt.

Afterwards the mutineers returned into the country so greatly discontented as they did not only rail on Monsieur de Hierges, the captain, and garrison, but on their king, general, and officers, in such sort that most of them swore they would be paid and better used or else they would serve the enemy against their king. The Duke of Alva, hearing their resolutions, dispatched commissioners to appease them and in the end was forced to content them both with five months' pay and assurance to be forgiven. Having pacified them and reconciled all, they accepted their officers and agreed to march whither they should be led. But first, according to their custom, every man gave a crown unto the *electo,* who was to depart with all speed out of the King's dominions but with good assurance and passport not to be molested.

This mutiny hindered the Duke of Alva's intent some month. Notwithstanding, according to his first resolution, Don Fadrique and Vitelli marched with all speed to enclose Alkmaar. So did the Duke follow with the rest in all speed. In the meantime the Prince and the States of Holland had sent into the town five or six expert captains, especially the Scottish men, Smith and Cornellys, who entered the town with some four hundred soldiers. The most of these captains had been in Haarlem and saved the town for a long time, next unto the Almighty's will. The vanguard being arrived, they soon engaged the town, so as none could either sally or enter.

The Duke of Alva, being arrived with the rest, prepared great pontoons or bridges with other necessaries to plant his battery, which he could hardly do by reason of the marsh and wet rotten grounds whereon the town stood. Notwithstanding, with his expert captains and cunning engineers he mounted eighteen pieces of cannon with some six culverins in a marshy ground against reason, impossible to be done as the defendants thought. These pieces did beat cross [100] on two platforms, a weak bulwark and a curtain some eight score off. Having no other flank by reason the ground served not, they could not bring the battery within less than eight score, wherefore their fury was the less. To say troth, all batteries ought to be placed within less than eight score; if it be full seven score it is very far to do any great hurt, in case the defendants be in any great numbers within, having store of earth to rampire and entrench themselves.

Notwithstanding, I heard some of the best defendants in that town say in their judgments the fear of the people and of most of the soldiers within was such that had not the enemies environed the town round about as they did, but left any place void, the best of the defendants would have quitted the place and shifted for themselves. But being straitly environed and no ways to escape, remembering their cruelty at Haarlem, they resolved to fight, by reason the soldiers which had been in Haarlem did importune the rest, especially the captains, who were assured to perish, coming into their enemy's hands.

After some seven thousand shot, the breach was reasonable, as the assailants thought; but in troth it was not, for above four foot of the ground of the rampire was nothing battered but falsely covered with the ruin of the parapet and the earth that fell from the highest parts of the breach. Also they were fain to give their assaults on pontoons and such engines, which they had made against reason to adventure men against a place defended with any valor; for a breach, be it made never so assaultable, having many hands to defend it with any valor, lightly is never entered, in case they within be of any judgment, as I said before, and having earth to entrench themselves. But the fury

[100] Crossfire.

of the Duke of Alva and his commanders was such that they advanced to the assault and attempted it with great courage. Being twice repulsed, notwithstanding, they advanced the third time to their folly and dear costs, for at those assaults they lost divers of their best captains and at the least 1,600 of their bravest soldiers.

The next day the rain fell in great abundance, in such sort that they raised their siege in few days, lost divers pieces of battery which they could not haul out of the marsh. At this town did the famous Duke of Alva lose the greatest credit that he did in any place since he carried arms, which he had done sixty years. For fifty years the least commandment he had was general of the horsemen, which place he had in Germany when Charles the Fifth overcame Duke John Frederick of Saxony and his confederates. But had the Duke marched straight to Delfshaven and taken it and Maaslandsluis when he marched to Alkmaar, which places were unfortified to any purpose, by all reason he had carried all Holland in a short time. I am sure the most men of war who know the seat of the country will confess no less than myself.

༄

Monsieur de Poyet surpriseth Gertruidenberg

Whilst the Duke of Alva was busy about his enterprise of Alkmaar, Monsieur de Poyet, who had been with Count Ludwig in Mons, being newly arrived out of France, was chosen lieutenant of the war to the Prince of Orange. Having conferred with the Prince, they gathered certain companies of English, Scottish, French, and Flemings at Dort in Holland, which they embarked with petards, ladders, and such engines of war. Monsieur de Poyet, using great diligence, landed his troops in the night on the dike toward Steenbergen, some half a league from the strong town of Gertruidenberg in Brabant, situated on the waterside next unto Dort. After placing his troops in order, he sent before him a valiant French captain named Malion, accompanied with a dozen resolute soldiers amongst whom were two or three of the country soldiers who had been often in the town and knew all the rampires as well as the inhabitants themselves. Whilst Malion spent some hour in discovering the place they meant to scale, Monsieur de Poyet advanced his troops toward the town. Being within a quarter of a league of the town, he stayed until about an hour before day. Having conferred with Malion, he delivered unto him some two hundred of his best soldiers, giving him charge to scale with all courage, assuring him to second him with the rest.

Malion and his troops entered the ditch of a small raveling [101] joining unto the rampire where he placed his ladders. After the passing of the round, notwithstanding that the sentinels gave the alarm, Malion and his troops recovered both raveling and rampire before any great troop came to encounter him. The garrison, being gathered together in reasonable numbers, charged Malion resolutely at the push of the pike but, being seconded by Monsieur de Poyet and his troops, they were quickly content to quit the fury and also forced to run into the market place whither the assailants followed them in the tail. Notwithstanding, being entered the market place, the Governor with his fresh troops turned upon us and gave a hot charge at the push of the pike; but our many hands soon overcame them, giving them the retreat in rout. Some took themselves into the townhouse, which they kept a little while and then yielded to have their lives saved. Divers ran over the rampire toward Breda. More than half were slain. The Governor with a few

---

[101] A raveling or ravelin was a triangular fortification projecting outward from the city wall.

recovered his house, which stood on the rampire, out of which he escaped over the wall unto Breda, leaving behind him all that he had saving what he carried upon him.

Thus was the strong town of Gertruidenberg surprised with less than 1,200 men, having in it at the last 600 soldiers besides burgesses, with the loss of 450 persons of our side, to the great grief of the Duke of Alva; not without reason, for, considering his loss and disgrace at Alkmaar, it did equal at the least his victory at Haarlem.

ಲ

Valdéz, sent by the Duke of Alva into Holland, entereth The Hague, attempteth Delft and other places without success

When the Duke of Alva advanced to besiege Alkmaar, he sent the master of his camp, Don Francisco de Valdéz, with his Tercio de la Ligue with five cornets of horsemen and some twelve companies of Walloons out of sundry regiments, commanding him to advance into the bowels of Holland to relieve his troops in the rich villages where he thought best, betwixt Leiden, Delft, and the seacoast as far as the river of Maas and the town of Brielle, charging him to attempt nothing without his advice and consent unless it were with sure intelligence with some of the towns.

Valdéz, being entered the fair and rich village of The Hague without any resistance, found it a place sufficient to lodge double his troops, all in covert and most in beds. This Hague is counted the fairest village in Europe and the place of the general assembly of all the Netherlands next unto Brussels, I mean the seventeen provinces since they were united under the house of Burgundy, where the King hath a fair palace and divers of the nobility houses, with a great multitude of lawyers. This

Valdéz Enters The Hague

Hague is such a village that Charles the Fifth, being requested to fortify it, answered he had rather it should remain the fairest village than a reasonable fair town. But I persuade myself both he and the country would have fortified it but that it standeth more than half on sandy grounds, which can never be made strong by the earth itself, by reason of the looseness of the sand. The Prince of Orange tried to do it but could not to any purpose, so as it might be kept with any garrison against an army, without a reasonable army to defend it.

Valdéz, after lodging a few days in The Hague, caused all the villages to bring him such necessaries as pleased him. Then he advanced certain of his companies to a village called Rijswijk in the way toward Leiden from Delft, which he entrenched and barricaded. Likewise he entrenched his first guards at the bridge half the way betwixt Delft and The Hague, where often our troops and theirs had many a hot skirmish, both near unto the guards and sometimes hard by the ports of Delft.

Colonel Morgan's regiment and divers companies of Frenchmen were lodged in the villages betwixt Delft and Rotterdam safely from the enemy, by reason both the towns covered them behind and before with great ditches on both sides, not to be passed with troops, having any guards to defend them. These troops served always ready to thrust into Delft, Rotterdam, Delfshaven, or Maaslandsluis where the enemy would have attempted first. In Leiden was Monsieur de Lorges, son to that brave Count of Montgomery, with a fair French regiment and other companies of Scots and of the countrymen and burgesses well armed. In Delft was Captain Chester with two hundred Englishmen, whom afterwards the Prince advanced to be colonel of those troops by reason of some sting against Colonel Morgan. There were in it also three fair companies of Frenchmen, besides the burgesses well armed. In Rotterdam were some bands of Scots and of the countrymen besides the burgesses. At Delfshaven was Monsieur de Maisonfleur with sundry

99

bands of French, Scots, and of the country. In Maaslandsluis was Monsieur de Saint Aldegonde and Treslong with some twelve hundred, most of them countrymen, a great number of peasants and burgesses. Besides, the garrisons wrought continually to fortify both Delfshaven and Maaslandsluis, in such sort that both the places were strong and guardable with reasonable defenses. Especially Delfshaven was very strong, not to be won easily, having necessaries that belong to a fortress. The garrison of Delfshaven had fortified the village of Overschie, half the way betwixt Delft and Rotterdam, where they kept a strong guard. Monsieur de Poyet, for the better assurance of Leiden, being the nearest place engaged and environed with enemies, thrust himself into it.

Valdéz practiced all he could with Leiden and Delft, once by treachery of some who kept the town port toward Utrecht. Valdéz prepared sundry turf boats in which he lodged good troops of soldiers. Once being entered the ports, with the resolution of the garrison and the good conduct of Poyet, they were repulsed, where Valdéz lost many of his men. Another time he had intelligence with some in Delft, but being discovered to the townsmen and garrison, divers of our bands which lodged hard by entered in the night, but either some of the townsmen or Valdéz' guards discovered our arming, so as he gave over his enterprise, when he was ready to attempt, in the like order as he did at Leiden; but had he come we were ready at the least a thousand soldiers, besides the burgesses, at the water-port where he should have entered, and had bent sundry pieces of artillery loaden with nails, hailshot, and such devices. Had he presented himself, his troops could not escape without great murder among them, with no danger to ourselves.

After these attempts Valdéz advertised the Duke of Alva of his affairs, showing him that no good could be done without an army and the fury of artillery. To that end he requested more troops or means, or leave to retire himself with those troops he had.

༖

The Duke of Alva retireth out of Holland, sendeth Julián Romero, Monsieur de Capres, and Fronsberg to assist Valdéz; Verdugo Governor of Haarlem

The Duke, remembering his disgrace at Alkmaar, fearing his army would mutiny if he would overcharge them with pains and travail, having no treasure to content them, resolved to retire to Brussels. But before he departed he sent the master of his camp, Julián Romero, to his army, which was lodged in the country by Utrecht and Amsterdam, giving him charge, if he could, to procure his Tercio of Lombardy, of which Julián [Romero] was colonel, to march into Holland to join with Valdéz. He sent also Monsieur de Capres, commanding him to procure his regiments of Walloons to do the like, also the regiment of Fronsberg the Almain. These colonels were directed to the camp to procure their regiments to march willingly and not perforce. He commanded Mendoza, general of his horsemen, to send with them six of the best cornets. After that, these regiments and cavalry were contented to enter Holland and had sworn to obey their colonels in all manner of service. The Duke of Alva gave the chief charge unto Julián [Romero], and the next unto him was Valdéz. He placed Colonel Verdugo Governor in Haarlem, with his regiment of Walloons and one cornet of horsemen, with three ensigns of Almains out of Fronsberg's regiment. Himself departed out of Amsterdam with his son Don Fadrique, Chiappino Vitelli, Mendoza, and all the rest of his army toward Brabant, resolving not to attempt any great siege or service before he had acquainted the King how the world went. To that end, being arrived at Brussels, he dispatched two of quality unto the King, either to send him treasure and means more plentifully and in better order or to give him leave to retire himself and to send another governor.

❧

Julián Romero winneth Maaslandsluis, but dareth not attempt Delfshaven

Julián [Romero] and his succors, being arrived and having conferred with Valdéz, resolved to attempt Maaslandsluis and dislodged from The Hague with their forces named before, haling with them six pieces of battery. Being arrived at the great village called Vlaardingen within a small league of Maaslandsluis, they quartered their horsemen with a regiment of footmen for their guards and departed with the rest to approach the Sluis. They carried with them all the *schuits* and boats that might be found, in wagons, with planks, ladders, and all other necessaries that they thought fit, to scale and to make bridges over the dikes. Being before the Sluis with their bridges and means they had made to pass the ditches, they took the great ditch on both sides of the Sluis, I mean the dike the Sluis stands upon and which keeps the sea from drowning the land. Having mounted their artillery on both sides of the dike, they dismounted ours within, which did beat on the dike. After turning their artillery toward the seas, I mean the river of Maas, which is above a league broad in that place, they beat away such vessels as the defendants had anchoring before their fort.

Monsieur de Treslong, being Admiral and Governor of Brielle, perceiving their success, departed out of the fort in a *schuit* with great hazard to recover Brielle. Presently the enemies passed their boats over the dike into the Maas. Being passed, it much abated the courage of Saint Aldegonde and his garrison, not without reason, for betwixt the fort and the water their rampire was worth nothing, so as at a high water it covered the dike of the fort as high as the parapet. The enemy, perceiving their success, prepared a pontoon which they builded artificially upon their boats and placed on it three of their pieces. The garrison, perceiving their stratagem, having no means to avoid it nor hope of succors, compounded for their fort, delivering the enemies their chief prisoners with their ensigns and arms.

Thus was the fort of Maaslandsluis lost, partly by reason our ships of war durst not hazard to dismount the enemy's artillery, which they might have done showing their accustomed valor, as they did since and before in divers places, but chiefly by reason our men did not cut the dike on both sides of the fort to have drowned the country. Having done that, the enemy would never have attempted the place. By reason of the strength of Delfshaven, the enemy refused to attempt it. To say troth, they had no reason to do it, having no means to approach but on such a dike, and the enemy being so well fortified and manned as their approaches had been vain.

ಶ್

The King of Spain calleth home the Duke of Alva and in his room establisheth Don Luis de Requesens Governor of the Low Countries

In this time order came from the King to retire the Duke of Alva into Spain and to resign his place unto Don Luis de Requesens, Comendador Mayor de Castile, a soldier of great reputation for counsel but nobody for execution, as the Battle of Lepanto could witness, for this Comendador, being chief coun-

selor to Don John of Austria, did what he could to procure the
Christian army not to hazard battle with the Turks. Also, being
in the fight, he advanced so slowly with a rear guard of galleys
that he nor his came to any blows, so as both there and in other
places always the Comendador was reputed a coward. But, belike in respect of his wit and mildness, the King sent him into
the Low Countries, perhaps persuaded that a mild captain
would win the hearts of the people far better with fair means
than the Duke of Alva with his cruelty. But in troth both King
and Council deceived themselves in calling away the Duke of
Alva and in making choice of such a general as the Comendador
Mayor, for by all reason, if the Duke had been royally maintained as he ought, he had made his master absolute king over
all the seventeen provinces. To say troth, fury and resolution
well used or executed had been the only ways to suppress that
nation, the Spanish being resolved to subdue them as they were.
For all other since, the witty, politic Netherlanders did always
overreach the Spanish, especially having such a head to direct
them as the Prince of Orange and being so strongly situated,
wanting no means to maintain wars and resolved to withstand
the Spanish to the uttermost rather than to yield to any composition. For whether the people be strongly situated or not, weal-
thy or poor, few or great in multitudes, being resolved to be mutinous and discontented, and not willing, as I said before, to be
brought unto any composition but such as pleaseth themselves,
God help that prince or state that must be forced to compound
with such a people by any means but by the sword, which had
been far more easy in the hands of the Duke of Alva than of the
poor Comendador; but the emulation amongst counselors for
greatness overthrew that service with many others, as I will
show hereafter. The Spanish priests, namely Cardinal Granvelle,
the Bishop of Toledo, with the aid of Ruy Gomez de Silva, did
persuade the King that the Duke of Alva was too great a subject. By such means rather than any other, the Duke of Alva was

called home and questioned for many disorders committed as well in other places as in the Low Countries.

❧

Walcheren besieged with the Prince's shipping; Middelburg relieved by the Spaniards; divers skirmishes betwixt the forces of either side; Mondragón entereth Middelburg; the Spanish navy at their return toward Antwerp defeated

Whilst Julián Romero was busy in Holland, Monsieur de Poyet and Boisot, Governor of Walcheren, with his brother, the Admiral of Zeeland, had besieged the island with a great number of ships of war, in such sort that nothing could enter into Middelburg, Arnemuiden, and Rammekens, which the enemies held. Monsieur de Beauvoir and Don Ruffello, being distressed for want of victuals in the said places, found means to acquaint the Comendador with their estate. Whereupon the Comendador sent for Julián Romero to come with most of his forces and to leave Valdéz with the rest in Holland. Having prepared a navy of some hundred sail of ships, hoys and crumsters, giving them in charge unto the masters of the camp, Sancho de Avila, castellan of Antwerp, and Mondragón, after furnishing them with all necessaries, both double manned with soldiers and appointed with great store of victuals, as well to relieve the distressed places as the army abroad, he commanded them to use all diligence, first to enter Middelburg and to relieve Mondragón, Governor of the island, with his regiment of Walloons and some four companies of Spaniards both with victuals and munition, then to return with the navy for Antwerp and to carry with them Monsieur de Beauvoir with his troops.

Before this navy passed Lillo, Messieurs de Poyet and Boisot had attempted the Rammekens and anchored with ships under the fort which did dismount divers pieces within, having their tops of musketproof out of which our musketeers did command the parapet next unto them. Also a mine was made in the dike toward Middelburg which being fired razed a corner of the fort, to little purpose but that there was but a few soldiers within, not half to man the walls, with a cowardly ensign-bearer which commanded. By these means the Rammekens was delivered to Monsieur de Poyet some four days before the succors arrived. Also there arrived from Holland Colonel Morgan and his regiment with other companies of Walloons and Flemings. The Spanish succors being in sight, our men planted the Spanish ensigns on the Rammekens and discharged a volley of artillery as if it were for joy, only to bring their navy to anchor under the commandment of our artillery. Being approached and anchored, they soon perceived what friends did welcome them. Instead of safe anchoring, they were fain to dislodge under the muck of the dike a league off to be safe from our artillery. Being anchored, Beauvoir and Ruffello marched with the most of their men of war to that place, haled with them four pieces of battery, which stood their navy in great stead, for they commanded all the road where the navy lay in such sort that albeit our navy anchored within half a league of theirs, betwixt them and Flushing, we durst not attempt them in that road by reason of their artillery mounted on the shore. Perceiving no hope to succor their distressed places by water, they took resolution to sail about the island and to land their men at a place named the Haaks, which stands on the neck of the island to the eastward from Veere, a league from the said town and some league and a half from Middelburg.

Whilst their navy was doubling about the island, our men of war marched right against them always, not knowing their intent nor where they meant to land; but had they known our directions, they might have easily entered and seized on the town of Flushing in sailing by it. Of two thousand soldiers which we had in the island, we had not in the town two hundred. In passing by Flushing, had their navy bent their course into the haven, there was nothing to defend them but a paltry boom, which God knows could never have endured one push of the smallest vessel. For the town artillery, it vexed them only in sailing by it. Being entered the haven, the soldiers had nothing to do but to have leaped out of their ships to shore on both sides of the haven, which might have been done easily, having nothing to let [102] them but the men of war, which were at their passing by a great league off, for then, God knows, the burgesses were nothing trained either with arms or any policy of defense. Also, at this instant the bulwark that flanked the haven was nothing furnished to any purpose. Therefore often true intelligence is the best part of an enterprise and worth always half an army.

Being anchored at the Haaks named before, they landed their men and placed on that dike certain pieces of artillery in like sort as they did at their last anchoring for defense of the navy. Having landed their victuals and such necessaries as they had to furnish their distressed places, they sent to Beauvoir and Ruffello to send them all the means they could to transport their necessaries. Being arrived, Mondragón's men with victuals and munition departed toward Middelburg, where, being arrived, Monsieur de Beauvoir and Don Ruffello returned with the old garrison to the Haaks. In this time all our men of war were arrived at Veere, the next place to front them, so was our navy anchored within half a league of theirs half the way betwixt the Haaks and Veere.

Monsieur de Rollé, Governor of the said town, having set good order in his town, Monsieur de Boisot, Governor of the whole island, and Rollé sallied with the rest to front the enemies at the Haaks. Being arrived right against our navy, we,

[102] Hinder.

being in number two thousand English, Scots, French, Walloons, and Flemings, entrenched our main [103] in that place. Then we advanced some 312 score further [104] and entrenched there two hundred, and advanced six score further one hundred. Our guard was narrow by reason we were entrenched on a dike of sixteen paces broad, the seas on the one side, on the other side meadows environed with ditches, not passable with armed men [105] without means to make bridges.

The enemies, perceiving our lodgings, belike thought it was to cut off their passage betwixt the Haaks and Middelburg. Whereupon, not having passed half their necessaries, presently, to intercept us, they marched full against us upon the dike; a thousand or more advanced into the meadows right against us; some five hundred on our side toward Middelburg followed with all their troops. Those on the dike forced our first troop to run, following them in rout unto our second. Being on the trench of our two hundred, we plagued them with a volley of shot, so as they were driven to retire about twelve score, where they stood until their shot [106] in the meadows approached near unto us. Colonel Morgan, perceiving the heat of their skirmish, advanced his lieutenant colonel, Captain Bingham, with two hundred shot and armed men. So did Boisot and Rollé advance with them and many of the other nations. Withal, the enemies advanced with great resolution upon the dike. So did the others in the meadows pass over the ditches with planks and hurdles in such manner that those troops annoyed us greatly, for they flanked us with volleys on our sides so cruelly that, being at the push of the pike with the troops on the dike, our men behind made away. The enemies, perceiving their retreat, passed over the trench, where they executed and hurt many by reason we fought and knew not of our fellows' retreat until our backs were toward the enemies, who followed us so close and with

[103] Our main body. [104] Six thousand two hundred and forty paces.
[105] Men in armor. [106] Musketeers.

such fury that our great stand ran about half a league until we came to a strong trench at a windmill, where we kept a good guard which was commanded by the town artillery. The enemy, perceiving the place too hot to attempt and not guardable being possessed, by reason of the town artillery, retired. We, perceiving their retreat, began to take such courage that we resolved to charge them, advancing with a cry and fresh resolution; charging their rear guard, their vanguard doubled their paces. Perceiving their countenances, it gave further courage, whereupon our charge began to be resolute and furious, so as all their troops ran, where we executed of them a far greater number than they did of ours in our first retreat. We followed them through their lost trenches close to their trench and village of Haaks.

By reason of the night's approach, we quitted our skirmish and kept guard at our trenches, which we mended all the night, keeping good guard and far better order than we did before. All the night both town and succors transported their necessaries into the town, so that by their great number of *schuits* and wagons all their victuals and necessaries were entered the town before two of the clock the next day in the afternoon; and as I said before, Mondragón with his entered Middelburg, and Beauvoir with Don Ruffello and their followers arrived at the Haaks. By reason of our equal losses and weariness, neither of both parties were eager to procure any skirmish, so that, according to the Comendador's directions, their troops embarked. Our fleet perceiving their meaning to sail for Antwerp, belike to discharge an honest report to the world, our chiefs resolved to fight with them by sea. Having taken resolution and embarked the most of our soldiers, we made toward them with good courage as they sailed by Veere.

Captain Yorke, being aboard the vice-admiral of Flushing with a great number of young English gentlemen and soldiers, the most of Colonel Morgan's company, procured our vice-admiral to board their vice-admiral, which he easily yielded unto, for the man was valiant and eager of himself to charge. So was valiant Monsieur de Boisot, our admiral, with the most or all his navy, very eager to charge their fleet, being well manned with good store of gallant soldiers of the nations of English, Scots, and French. Being close together, with great courage ours cried amain.[107] According to direction, our vice-admiral boarded theirs. So did valiant Robinson, a Scottish captain, being in one of the best Flushingers, board their rear admiral. Monsieur Boisot charged their admiral through their navy, who escaped with good sailing. Captain Henri and Ambroise le Duc, the valiant Frenchmen and Walloons being aboard of some of our best sails, boarded also two of their best sorts of vessels. The enemy, perceiving our resolution, fell in rout before the wind with all the sails they could make to recover the river of Antwerp. Notwithstanding, we took, burned, and forced to run on the sands above two-and-thirty sails and returned victorious with their vice-admiral, rear admiral, and divers others into our town of Veere, where we filled our prisons with Spaniards, Walloons, and great numbers of their mariners.

This victory recompensed in honor double theirs, although not so profitable as their victualing of Middelburg and Arnemuiden, which by that means held out many a month the longer and would have done still but for the defeat of Reimerswaal. Notwithstanding that Middelburg was victualed and far better manned, principally by the person of brave Colonel Mondragón, the Prince gave not over his determined purpose but charged both the Boisots, I mean the Governor and his brother the Admiral, to use all diligence to make sure guard round about the island with their ships, as they did before, and to cut off all succors from entering any more. To that end they prepared a far greater number both of ships and soldiers, on which enterprise

[107] In full force of numbers.

the Prince did set his rest with good reason, for he was assured to win the island in time, being master on the seas.

Within few months, Mondragón and his began to fall into distress for want of victuals. To terrify them the more, the Prince sent his lieutenant general, Monsieur de Poyet, into Walcheren with the most of his men of war, saving Colonel Morgan's regiment, which remained in Strinland,[108] standing on terms for pay and leave to return for England by reason of some discourtesies that fell out betwixt the Prince and the officers of the said regiment. Notwithstanding, divers gentlemen of that regiment accompanied Monsieur de Poyet, amongst others Captain Walter Morgan, Master Christopher Carleill, and Master Anthony Fant. Mondragón, fearing Poyet would attempt Arnemuiden, sent his lieutenant colonel into the said town with a strong guard, by reason the place was but newly fortified but very strong, without many hands to defend it. Also he kept a strong guard at the head of Middelburg a mile out of the town to defend the haven.

Poyet advanced his forces on the Rammekens dike toward Middelburg. Being arrived right against the enemy's guards at the head, ours entrenched themselves in that place, lodging our forces on the dike from the Rammekens to the said first guard, having betwixt us and the enemy the haven which might be some three score broad, where we had divers good skirmishes as well by those that sallied from Middelburg as by them that lodged at the head.[109]

---

[108] Land of Strijen.

[109] Middelburg is a short distance inland but is connected by a waterway with an arm of the Scheldt. Williams probably means at the head of this waterway.

The occasion of Sir Roger Williams serving the Spaniard

Colonel Morgan being arrived in England with his regiment in good order to the number of seven hundred, who being mustered before Her Majesty near to St. James, the Colonel and some four hundred of his best men were sent into Ireland, which in truth were the first perfect harquebusiers that were of our nation and the first troops that taught our nation to like the musket, as I said in my little discourse of the Spanish discipline. There also I touch how Philip de Comines speaks much of Louis the Eleventh but nothing how he quitted his Duke of Burgundy. Most true it is, at Colonel Morgan's going into Ireland, hearing how the young Prince of Condé was newly escaped from France into Germany, meaning, as it was told me, to levy an army and to march with all speed into France, this bruit [110] and my greedy desires to travel to see strange wars made me to quit the voyage into Ireland and to go with all speed toward the said Prince. Being arrived in Germany, I found the Prince nothing ready to march, nor any speech of his sudden levy. Having spent there all the time I could, want of crowns forced me to return for England.

Passing from Cologne toward Antwerp and entering Lier in Brabant, I was brought before the master of the camp, Julián Romero, who amongst many questions inquired of me what noblemen in England I knew best. I answered, the Earl of Pembroke, whom I served a page. He replied, "What? He that was general of the English before Saint-Quentin? I never honored any man more," and withal requested me earnestly to try his courtesy in the Spanish army, assuring me to depart when [it] pleased me. Having spent all my crowns, and being loath to return into England without seeing something, I promised to stay. Also, in those days there was no dispute betwixt Her Majesty

[110] Rumor.

and the Spanish king, to my knowledge. This was the manner
and the first hour that I entered into the Spanish service.

ᔇ

*Middelburg in distress; the Spanish prepare a navy to
relieve it, which is beaten and overthrown by the
Nassauians in a furious conflict*

Mondragón, feeling his wants, advertised the Comendador,
who perceiving no means to succor him but by sea, which could
not be without forcing the Prince's ships, prepared all the sails
and means he could. In time, he made ready some 120 sail, of
which were fourscore of war, as well ships as crumsters and
hoys, the rest victualers laden with all necessaries to furnish
the distressed places. Being in readiness, some at Antwerp,
some at Bergen-op-Zoom, the rest at Goes, he gave them in
charge to his masters of camp, Julián Romero and Sancho de
Avila, desiring them for fashion sake to accept Monsieur de
Beauvoir for admiral and to give him some grace in respect of
his disabling for the commandment of Zeeland. This he did only
to flatter the Walloons, by reason Monsieur de Beauvoir was
descended from one of their principal houses.

The Prince, hearing their intent, prepared for his navy all or
the most of the ships of war that Holland and Zeeland could
make at that time to the number of some two hundred, a few
ships, the rest crumsters and hoys. These are the best ships to
fight in those waters by reason the most of them draw but little
water and carry for the most part principal good artillery, some
demicannons, and many whole culverins; [111] for those waters

[111] At this period the culverin was the heaviest gun in general use. A
demicannon was also a heavy gun with a bore of approximately seven
inches.

are full of sands and many dangers, although it be broad in some places ten of our miles, all covered with seas, notwithstanding not navigable in the most places but in narrow streams, insomuch as in many places you may discover steeples and banks which in time past were islands like unto the rest. For this cause, I suppose, those countries do carry the name of Sealand.[112] Also, those small sails turn far shorter and readier than other ships in those narrow passages and keep far better by a wind. Having this navy in a readiness, well manned, especially with great store of good mariners, besides a good number of soldiers of Scots, French, and Netherlanders, he commanded his admiral, Monsieur de Boisot, to advance with his navy betwixt Zierikzee and Goes where the enemies must pass, there to try the fortune of war, rather than they should succor Mondragón.

After finishing all preparations, the Comendador divided his navy named before into three squadrons. The greatest vessels and the far more in number he commanded Sancho de Avila to advance under the island of Goes, there to anchor under the favor of some artillery mounted on the shore and to stay in readiness until he received further direction. Himself with the rest of his council and army marched to Bergen-op-Zoom, where he found Julián Romero and his admiral, Beauvoir, ready to set out with the rest of his navy, staying but for his directions. He divided their vessels into two squadrons, giving them equally to the admiral and Julián Romero. All his navy being furnished to the uttermost he could, they wanted mariners, especially of the same countrymen that were well acquainted with those sands and shallow waters; but they were very well manned with brave land soldiers, for they had in them some ninety ensigns of soldiers, Spanish, Burgundians, and Walloons.

The Comendador, after placing himself with his nobility and a great troop of men of war on the high bank of Brabant within

[112] Williams is here translating the name Zeeland.

half a league of Bergen, where he might see very easily the place where the battle was fought, having given a signal to Sancho de Avila from a hill on Brabant side which he might easily perceive, Sancho de Avila advanced his squadron with all the sails he could toward Reimerswaal, where the Nassauians lay in good order of battle, having divided their battle into four squadrons. Monsieur de Boisot, the Admiral of Zeeland, commanded the greatest; the Admiral of Holland the second, which was his right wing; the Admiral of Zierikzee the third, which was the left wing. Boisot's vice-admiral, Boenire,[113] commanded the fourth, whom Boisot commanded to make all the sails he could toward Sancho de Avila. Being arrived within culverin shot, he commanded Boenire to lead Sancho de Avila over the shallow waters if he would follow him; if not, to keep in the wind as near unto him as he could without fighting, unless the enemy would force him, until Boisot began.

Julián [Romero] and Beauvoir, having not two leagues to sail unto the Nassauians, who were ready under the head of Bergen in good order, and perceiving that Sancho de Avila could not sail unto them by reason that most of his vessels drew too deep water and that his smallest vessels were in fight with Boenire, they advanced with great courage in good order, thinking to have sailed betwixt the Nassauians and Brabant side and to have joined with Sancho de Avila. By this time Sancho de Avila's smallest vessels were in hot skirmish with Boisot's vice-admiral, but many of his greatest vessels were run on ground with very ambition to come to fight before their fellows, Julián [Romero] and Beauvoir being right against the Nassauians. Boisot, having the wind, made with all resolution toward the enemy; so did they abide them with no less courage, in such sort that the valiant admiral, Monsieur de Boisot, and the res-

[113] It is difficult to identify Boenire. This may be a corruption of Bouwen Ewoutsz.

olute master of the camp, Julián Romero, boarded each other. So did the Admiral of Zierikzee and the Admiral Beauvoir board each other with no less courage.

So did Boenire, Boisot's vice-admiral, board the vice-admiral of Sancho de Avila. Being in wonderful hot fight a long time, the most part of the vessels, especially the squadrons of Julián Romero and Boisot, had been on aboard each other near two hours, the most part of which time they were at the push of the pike and blows of swords. Boisot and his fellows were more expert seamen than the Spanish commanders and far better furnished with all manner of provisions that belong to a sea fight, especially fireworks, which they employed to the Spaniards' great loss, so that Julián Romero's *alférez*, being aboard of Boisot, was blown up with powder, and with him threescore at the least of his bravest soldiers. And had they not done it at that instant, Julián Romero himself had been gone, for he was entering with the rest. The Spaniards were cruelly plagued in all quarters, especially by reason Sancho de Avila's great vessels could not come to succor their fellows among which he was in person, being a most valiant man, accompanied with a great number of their best soldiers. Julián Romero, perceiving his fellows distressed without remedy and himself most of all, with wonderful hazard he and divers of his gentlemen and soldiers did leap into their *schuits*, which carried them to the shore where the Comendador stood. So did many others escape by the like means. Likewise divers of their smallest vessels ran themselves on the shore where the Comendador stood. Many were fast on the sands; divers were burned. The rest made all the sails they could to recover the river of Antwerp. Amongst these was Sancho de Avila, notwithstanding he had grounded his own vessel in seeking to come to fight. The Nassauians followed them into the river of Antwerp, defeating and taking many as they ran away.

By the Spaniards' own reports, they lost in this battle above threescore sail of all sorts, forty-seven ensigns, above six hundred brass pieces, of which above two hundred were taken out of the citadel of Antwerp, slain and taken above six thousand soldiers and mariners. Few were saved that came to their hands, but all or the most that were taken were slain or drowned. Amongst many of their commanders and men of good account, their Admiral Beauvoir was slain valiantly at the push of pike. So was Sancho de Avila's vice-admiral. The victorious escaped not scot-free, for their Admiral Boisot lost his right eye with the blow of a pike, the Admiral of Holland sore hurt with a shot in the thigh. Boenire, Boisot's vice-admiral, was slain with many other[s] of good mark, besides at the least sixteen hundred soldiers and mariners.

Thus was the Battle of Reimerswaal begun and ended. Perhaps some will say because there was no greater slaughter and confusion it may not be termed worthy and comparable unto divers others. But in troth I heard divers report, besides the Comendador, who had been at Lepanto and here, that the fury there was nothing comparable unto this, number to number. For my part, I never saw anything so furious. I may well speak it, for there are some of good quality yet alive can testify the same. But for Julián Romero himself, I had been blown up with his *alférez*, yet I escaped with as great hazard as any other of his followers.[114] But I will dispute against any soldier that no fight hath been comparable unto it by sea these five hundred years, saving that before Sluis, fought by our famous King Edward the Third against the French king and the Earl of Flanders, and that of Lepanto.

[114] From these remarks it is apparent that in this battle Williams fought on the Spanish side.

Principal Persons Mentioned in the Text

Adolf of Nassau (1540–1568)

He was the fourth son of William the Rich, Count of Nassau, and Juliana van Stolberg, and thus a younger brother of William of Orange.

Alva or Alba. Fernando Alvarez de Toledo, Duke of Alva (1508–1582)

A distinguished soldier and statesman of Philip II, Alva was appointed Captain General in the Netherlands in 1567. Subsequently he became also Regent and Governor General. He attempted to suppress the rebellion in the Netherlands by a policy of frightfulness and set up a court at Brussels, popularly known as the Council of Blood, for the trial of heretics and traitors. Some 18,000 people were executed during Alva's regime, including Egmond and Hoorne. He was recalled to Spain in 1573.

Arenberg (or Aremberg). Jean de Ligne, Count of Arenberg (1525–1568)

Arenberg, a Knight of the Golden Fleece, was a member of an important family of Hainaut. In 1547 he married an heiress, Margaretha van der Marck, Countess of Arenberg, and thereby acquired the title of Count of Arenberg. He served under Maximiliaan van Egmond in the Schmalkaldic war and was his successor on January 1, 1549, as Stadholder (in effect, Governor) of Friesland, Overijssel, Groningen, Drente, and from 1551 Lingen also. In the war of Philip II against France, he took part in the Battle of Saint-Quentin and in 1559 was made a field marshal. Originally he stood well with the rebellious great nobles such as Egmond, Orange, and Hoorne; but his relations with Margaret of Parma, the Regent or Governess of the Netherlands, were also cordial. Arenberg, by temperament, sought to avoid extreme measures whenever possible. He strove, for example, for moderation in the framing of the laws against heretics and attempted to soften the proceedings of the Inquisition. He remained true to

121

the Catholic faith and did not come out firmly for the League of Nobles and against Cardinal Granvelle, as did nearly all other Stadholders. Yet when Montigny went to Spain, he received, while still in Spain, instructions and documents from his fellow members of the League of Nobles. Among these papers was one attesting the fact that Arenberg was a member of the League. He was never an active or enthusiastic member, and upon the insistence of his brother-in-law, Aerschot, the head of the powerful family of Croy, he gradually withdrew from League activities. In 1566, together with Count Meghen, Arenberg was active in raising troops to check the disturbances which followed the activities of the League of Nobles and the image-breaking. In his own provinces, he restored the wavering authority of the crown and the Catholic religion. He was at that time a member of the Council of State.

When the Duke of Alva arrived in the Netherlands in 1567, Arenberg took service under him, and in November of that year he was sent to France with 1,500 reiters to help Charles X against Condé. Upon his return to the Netherlands and at the time of the incursion of Louis of Nassau into Groningen, Arenberg, as Governor of Groningen, moved to expel Louis. With Meghen, Stadholder of Gelderland, Arenberg took over command of the campaign and was joined by a contingent of Spanish troops under Bracamonte. In his subsequent defeat at Heiligerlee, Arenberg slew Adolf of Nassau with his own hand; he was himself killed by Antonie de Zoete, Lord of Haultain.

Arenberg was regarded by those loyal to Philip II as a gallant commander, a cultivated gentleman, and a prudent administrator.

Avila. Sancho de Avila, or Sancho Davila (1523–1583)

Avila was a well-known and talented Spanish officer. He came to the Netherlands in 1567 as captain of the life guards of the Duke of Alva. He is known to many as the man who took Hoorne and Egmond into custody. In 1568 he achieved a notable victory over the forces of the Prince of Orange near Daelhem. Between 1572 and 1574 he fought in Zeeland. In April and May of 1572 he managed to relieve Middelburg and also to take Arnemuiden from the Sea Beggars. In the same year, in collaboration with

Mondragón, he made an effort to relieve Goes, but on October 21, 1572, he was compelled to break off that effort. Despite their most strenuous endeavors, Mondragón's troops and Avila's ships were unable to free Zeeland ports and waters from the control of the Sea Beggars.

When, in the spring of 1574, Ludwig of Nassau planned to invade Limburg and Gelderland, Avila anticipated that Ludwig would cross the Maas somewhere between Maastricht and Roermond. Avila met Ludwig's forces at Mook on the right bank of the Maas on April 14, 1574. Although Ludwig of Nassau's forces far outnumbered his own, Avila had chosen his ground carefully and inflicted a severe defeat on his enemy. Both Ludwig of Nassau and his brothers Henry and Christopher were killed in the encounter.

Subsequently Avila was commander of the Citadel at Antwerp. In November, 1576, there was a clash between the Spanish troops, largely mutineers, in the Citadel and the troops in the city, who were under the control of the States-General. The Spanish made a sortie from the Citadel and Avila was unable to restrain them. The mutinous Spanish entered upon a frightful orgy of plunder and slaughter which has since been known as the Spanish Fury. After leaving the Netherlands, Avila fought under his old chief, the Duke of Alva, in Portugal (1580–1583). At the conquest of Oporto (October 24, 1580) he completed the subjugation of Portugal for Philip II. He died at Lisbon in 1583 as the result of infected wounds.

Baerland, or Baarland, or Barland, or Berland. Jacobus Smit, Lord of Baerland

As Williams indicates, Baerland was Baily of Flushing. François le Petit, in *La grande chronique . . . de Hollande, Zelande* (Dort, 1601), II, 252, says under the date of June 10, 1573, that "on the tenth about eleven o'clock at night died the Seigneur de Berlant, Governor and Baily of Flushing, a person who loved his country and was diligent in his office. And because of the affection which he had for them, the bourgeois and mariners of Flushing did a great deal. The current rumor was that he had been poisoned by a woman whom he had lodged in his house."

Principal Persons Mentioned

Balfour

There were three persons named Balfour who fought in the Netherlands in these years. They were:

Bartholomew, who in 1585 was Governor of Bergen-op-Zoom and colonel of a regiment of Scottish troops. In 1587 he was commandant at Arnhem. He took part in many important actions and always behaved courageously. When Hulst was besieged by the Spanish in 1596, Balfour was among the defenders and was killed in a Spanish attack on that city. *Sir Henry* was a brother of Bartholomew. On January 28, 1573, he entered beleaguered Haarlem. On the evening of April 19, commanding a company of three hundred soldiers, he forced an entrance into the blockhouse of Rustenberg and captured it. It remained in his hands until the end of the siege. After the capitulation of Haarlem, Balfour was granted his life on condition that he would murder the Prince of Orange, but on obtaining his freedom he related to the Prince of Orange the conditions under which he had been released and remained loyal to the Prince thereafter. He was colonel of a regiment of Scottish troops and was killed in 1580 in the vicinity of Bruges. His son was called *Guillaume* (F. J. S. Ten Raa and François de Bas, *Het Staatsche Leger* [Breda, 1911], I, 266–267).

Barberini, Rafaelo Barberini

Williams writes this name "Don Ruffello," but there seems little doubt that he means Barberini. Cardinal Bentivoglio, in his *History of the Wars of Flanders* (London, 1678), book VIII, p. 111, says that "of the Italian nobility which were then in the army of Flanders, Rafell Barberini was in great esteem and was much employed in many weighty actions." Barberini was a capable engineer and a great mathematician. He was with the army of Alva in 1568 and took part in the important actions of that year. In the following year, the Portuguese ships returning from India laden with merchandise were captured by the English. At the behest of Philip II, Alva sent an embassy to England to see if an accord could be reached with the English, and Barberini was a member of that embassy. The diplomatic endeavor achieved nothing. In 1574 Barberini took part in the campaigns in Zeeland and reported their day-by-day events. (See Jacob Presser, *De*

124

tachtigjarige Oorlog [Amsterdam, 1948], p. 7.) It may be noted that Famiano Strada says that parts of his account of the actions in Groningen are taken from letters which Rafaelo Barberini sent home to Italy. (See Strada's *History of the Low Country Wars* [London, 1667], VI, 60.)

There appears to have been no other commander on the Spanish side with the Christian name of Rafael with the exception of Rafael Manrique, who was not prominent in the actions discussed by Williams.

Batenburg. Willem van Bronkhorst, Lord of Batenburg and Stein (died July 10, 1573)

Batenburg was a personal enemy of Alva and a devoted follower of the Prince of Orange. His manors had been confiscated by the officers of Philip II in 1569. In 1572 the Prince of Orange sent him to Zeeland to stimulate the revolt there, and in that year and the year following he was the Prince's lieutenant general in Zeeland. In 1573 he followed Lumey as commander of the forces sent to relieve Haarlem, and in the same year, together with Marinus Brandt, he was defeated in the crucial battle on the Haarlemmermeer. After several subsequent unsuccessful actions he made a final effort to relieve Haarlem at the beginning of July, 1573. On July 8 he marched his troops from the village of Sassenheim toward Haarlem and marched them straight into an ambush. Batenburg was badly wounded, taken prisoner, and died shortly thereafter. His death was not greatly lamented. It was commonly thought that the chief reason for the failure of his enterprises was a too great indulgence in alcohol.

Beauvoir. Philippe de Lannoy, Lord of Beauvoir or Beauvais (died 1574)

Lannoy was a distinguished soldier on the Spanish side during the wars in the Netherlands. In 1562 Lannoy was commandant of Hesdin. In 1566 Margaret of Parma sent him to Doornik to defend the position of the government and church against Hoorne. In 1567 he defeated an attempt by the Sea Beggars to seize Walcheren. He also defeated the troops of Jan van Marnix, Lord of Toulouse, at Austruweel (near Antwerp) on March 13, 1567. He was Governor of Flushing and Middelburg and made every effort to keep those cities loyal to the King of Spain. He occupied Arnemuiden in June, 1572, but a month later was defeated by Tseraerts at Zoutelande. In 1573 he outfitted a fleet to bring back the cities of Zeeland to loyalty to Spain, but the effort was unsuccessful. Beauvoir later commanded a fleet whose object was to provision Middelburg, but this effort was also unsuccessful.

Bergen. Jan IV van Glymes, Marquis of Bergen (1528–1567)

In 1555 Bergen was made a Knight of the Golden Fleece and in 1559 Stadholder of Hainaut. He stood next to Orange in importance in the group of nobles opposing the central government. He was a capable and steadfast man and for that reason was feared and slighted by Granvelle. In 1560 he was made Stadholder of Valenciennes, a position of no great importance. Valenciennes being near the French border, there was great activity among the Protestants of the city in importing Calvinist preachers from France, and it was known that Bergen winked at this. Granvelle also complained of the unusually slack enforcement by Bergen of the edicts against heretics. In 1562 Bergen supported the sending of Montigny to Spain. Later, in 1566, he and Montigny went to Spain as representatives of the League of Nobles to lay before Philip II a true picture of conditions in the Netherlands. The two achieved nothing and Bergen died at Segovia, sick and discouraged. In 1570 his property was confiscated by the Council of Blood upon the orders of Alva, although during his life Bergen had remained true to the Catholic faith.

Bergh. Willem, Count van den Bergh (1537–1586)

Van den Bergh was married to Maria, the eldest sister of the Prince of Orange. He was at first devoted to helping his brother-in-law and was a member of the League of Nobles. He fortified his castles when the trouble began, but when, in May, 1567, all resistance was broken, he was forced to flee to Bremen. He was accused and summoned to appear before the Council of Blood. When he did not appear, his numerous properties were confiscated. At this time he was in close touch with both Orange and Brederode. In 1570 he was instrumental in the attack on Loevestein and the taking of the castle by Herman de Ruiter, and he also made an effort to surprise Deventer. After the Sea Beggars had taken

Principal Persons Mentioned

Brielle, van den Bergh engaged in a number of actions and campaigns, none of which was very successful.

When Zutphen fell into the hands of the Spanish, van den Bergh fled to Cologne and remained there until the Pacification of Ghent in 1576. In 1577 he returned to Gelderland, and by 1580 he must already have been in secret communication with Parma. In 1581, with the support of the many royalists, he managed to have himself named by the States as successor to Jan van Nassau as Stadholder of Gelderland. Van den Bergh hung between the two parties, Parma on the one hand and the States on the other, but the fact that the very trustworthy Leoninus, Chancellor of Gelderland, remained at his post appeared to be sufficient guarantee that van den Bergh would remain loyal to the States. Actually he did his duty, but he was continually urged by Parma to go over to the side of Spain. Van den Bergh did not wholly repulse these urgings, for he hoped to gain some advantage for himself and his family. A suspicious correspondence between him and Parma was discovered in November, 1583. The Count and his family were immediately taken into custody and van den Bergh was imprisoned in Delfshaven for a year. The treason of van den Bergh was naturally a great blow to William of Orange. In March, 1584, van den Bergh was set at liberty, with several conditions attached to that freedom. He established himself at Emmerik and in October, 1584, broke his word to the States that he would remain neutral. He thereby cut the remaining ties which had bound him to the side of William of Orange. The few years which remained to him he spent in rendering assistance to the party of Philip II and in endeavoring to induce others to defect from the side of the Netherlanders and join the Spanish party.

Berlaymont. Gilles van Berlaymont, Count of Hierges (died June 18, 1579)

Gilles was the eldest son of Karel, Count of Berlaymont, who was more prominent than his son. After the outbreak of iconoclasm Gilles was commissioned by the Regent to recruit and command a regiment. He took part in the siege of Valenciennes in 1567 and was a member of the infamous Council of Blood or Council of Troubles. In 1572 he was named a Knight of the Golden Fleece and Stadholder of Friesland. Shortly thereafter he was also named Stadholder of Gelderland. He was not present at the siege of Haarlem in 1573, since at that time he was defending Gelderland against the troops of the Prince of Orange while the Spanish troops were occupied with the siege of Haarlem. He was at Mook in 1574. When Bossu was taken prisoner, Berlaymont succeeded him as Stadholder of Holland, Zeeland, and Utrecht. As commander of the forces of Spain, he conquered Oudewater in 1575. He served under Don John after the latter's arrival in the Netherlands and was at the surprise attack on Namur. He conquered Charlemont for the Regent when he was general of artillery and negotiated with the Holland cities in the name of Don John. He was also a member of the Council of State. In 1578 he followed his father as chief of finances and as Stadholder of Namur, but before he could assume these functions he died at the siege of Maastricht. His younger brother, Claude de Berlaymont, Baron de Haultpenne (1555–1587), was also an officer under Don John and under Parma. About 1585 he was Governor of Breda and in 1585–1587 Stadholder of Gelderland.

Bernaert. Niklaes Bernaert

In 1572 he commanded a company of soldiers raised in England among the refugee Netherlanders and was one of the Sea Beggars who captured Brielle. He took part in many important actions in Zeeland and in 1573 was in beleaguered Haarlem. During the siege, Captain Niklaes Bernaert and four men succeeded in getting out of the city in a small boat, carrying a message to the Prince of Orange asking that he bring help to the city (J. W. Wijn, *Het Beleg van Haarlem* [Amsterdam, 1942], p. 186). In 1575 Bernaert was still in the army of the States.

Bingham, or Byngham. Sir Richard Bingham (1526–1599)

Bingham was a soldier with long years of experience before he took part in the Netherlands wars. In 1557, while in the service of Philip II, he fought against the French at the Battle of Saint-Quentin. He fought with the Spanish and the Venetians against the Turks under Don John of Austria and appears to have taken part in the conquest of Cyprus and the Battle of Lepanto (1572). In 1573–1574 he fought in the Netherlands on the side of the Prince.

In 1576, together with Sir Edward Horsey, he took part in an abortive mission to Don John of Austria to arrange a peace between Spain and the States-General. In 1578 he was in the army of William of Orange, but in 1579 he was sent to Ireland to aid in putting down the Desmond insurrection. He fought again in the Netherlands in 1587–1588 with the English expeditionary force. In addition to his career as a soldier, he had a distinguished and eventful career as Governor of Connaught and was knighted while holding that office. See the *D.N.B.*

Blois. Willem van Blois called Treslong, Lord of Oudenhoorn, Grysoort, and Petegem in Flanders (1529–1594)

Blois was the son of the Baily of Brielle and Voorne. He entered the royal sea service in 1556. He followed Charles V to Spain, was with Admiral Boshuizen in Denmark, and fought against the French and Turks. He eventually became a militant Calvinist and joined the forces of the Prince of Orange in the Netherlands wars. He was a member of the League of Nobles, took part in the image-breaking at The Hague, entered the service of Brederode, and was among the originators of the attempt on Amsterdam. In 1567 he took refuge at Emden and in 1568 fought on the side of the rebels at Heiligerlee and Jemmingen, being badly wounded in the latter battle. He then took service under Count Edzard of East Friesland. In 1568 Alva declared him banished for the rest of his life. Fitting out his own ship, he joined the Sea Beggars and in 1571 plundered the coast in both West and East Friesland. He was active along the Dutch coast in 1572 also, and in the same year was Captain General of the Sea Beggars. In this command, together with Lumey, he organized the attack on Brielle. Thereafter he was Baily and Dike-reeve of the land of Voorne. In 1573 he became Admiral of Holland and in 1576 Admiral of Zeeland. In 1585 he was at Middelburg as admiral of the fleet which was intended to relieve Antwerp. In this same year Blois became involved in quarrels with members of his admiralty concerning the manner in which affairs with England were to be handled. Charges were brought against him; he was imprisoned but speedily restored to honor. This episode took place at the time of the fall of Antwerp (August, 1585). As a reward for his many services, in 1592 he was named by Maurits as Lieutenant

129

Forester and in 1593 as Falconer, but he had little interest in these honorary positions. Thereafter King Karel of Sweden commissioned him to raise a regiment of auxiliary troops for service with Sweden, but this commission came to nothing. He spent his last days at his country home of Zwieten near Leiden and died there in 1594.

Boisot. Charles de Boisot, Lord of Huysingen (1530–1575)

This South Netherlands nobleman was a member of the League of Nobles, but at the end of 1566 he hesitated to give it further support. Like so many others, he fled the country in 1567 and was accused before the Council of Blood in 1568. Both he and his wife were declared banished and their goods and property confiscated. He established himself in exile at Cologne and from that time forward was a follower of the Prince of Orange. The Prince sent him on a mission to Queen Elizabeth and in 1573 appointed him Governor of Flushing. In that year he fought in Waterland and Zeeland against the Spanish. He tried without success to take Middelburg but did make himself master of the fortress of Rammekens. In 1573 he also took part in the vain effort to relieve Haarlem. A second effort against Middelburg in the following year, 1574, succeeded, and he took not only that city but Arnemuiden as well. In 1575, as a member of the commission appointed for the purpose, Boisot had an important part in the settlement or definition of the power of the Prince in Holland and Zeeland (July 11, 1575). He was also present at the peace negotiations at Breda, March–July, 1575. He was killed September 30, 1575, when the Spanish troops under Mondragón invaded Zeeland (Schouwen and Duiveland).

Boisot. Louis de Boisot, Lord of Ruart (1528–1576)

A brother of Charles Boisot and until 1567 one of the court nobility at Brussels, he entered the sea service and apparently neither took part in the disturbances of 1566 nor signed the pact of the League of Nobles. Nevertheless he fled the country in 1567 and in that year entered the service of the Prince of Orange. He took part in the Prince's campaign across the Maas in 1572. Immediately before the Eve of St. Bartholomew, the Prince sent him with an important commission to Coligny, but he was apprehended and imprisoned. Until the spring of 1573 he was in custody but then fled to England. He was back in Holland that same year and took part in the vain effort to relieve Haarlem. In 1573 also, he was named Admiral of Zeeland by the Prince of Orange, and in the following year he was made Lieutenant Admiral of Holland and Zeeland. In this year, 1574, he scored a brilliant victory over the fleet of Requesens at Reimerswaal, a victory that was of decisive importance for the fall of Middelburg. In 1574 also he headed expeditions to get supplies into beleaguered Leiden, and beginning in that year he was also a member of the "Provincial Council" of Zeeland.

Upon him rested the primary responsibility for the defense of Zeeland against the Spanish. With Flushing as his base, he operated against the fleets of Mondragón and Sancho de Avila. He was killed in an effort to relieve Zierikzee, May 27, 1576.

Bossu or Boussu. Maximiliaan de Hennin (or Henin-Liétard), Count of Bossu (1542–1578)

Bossu was a member of a well-known Hainaut family. In 1556 he was a member of the Council of State and in 1559 commander of a band of ordnance. He was a friend of Granvelle and stood by the Cardinal against the League of Nobles. After William of Orange fled to Dillenburg in 1567, Bossu was appointed in his place as Stadholder over Holland, Zeeland, and Utrecht. When Brielle fell (1572), he marched with his troops by way of South Holland to recapture the city, his advance being everywhere retarded by great resistance. He was compelled to turn away from the line of march to Dort, where he supported Don Fadrique in his effort to punish that rebellious city. In this same year he took both Rotterdam and Amersfoort. In the siege of Haarlem he scored an important victory on the Haarlemmermeer (May 28, 1573) which doomed Haarlem.

In October, 1573, a few days after the relief of Alkmaar, in the battle on the Zuider Zee, he was defeated and taken prisoner. While in prison he had a change of heart and joined the party of William of Orange. After obtaining his freedom as a result of the Pacification of Ghent, he was one of those who worked to bring about the Union of Brussels (January 9, 1577). He did not join with Don John of Austria but remained true to the States-General and took part in the naming of Matthias as Regent. After Gembloux

Principal Persons Mentioned

(January 31, 1578) Bossu defended Brussels, took part in the Battle of Rymenam and remained after that as commander in chief of the States army at Antwerp, where he became ill and died.

Bouser and MacWilliams

Bouser was killed in a sortie out of Flushing against the Spanish troops who operated from Middelburg. Thomas Churchyard, *A General Rehearsal of Wars*, 1579 (STC 5235), K4 recto, implies that MacWilliams was killed about the same time as Bouser. Churchyard says, "Sir Humphrey Gilbert in this season (with a good number of soldiers and English gentlemen) was at Flushing and served well in those parts, and one Captain Morgan and Master Cotton, a Pensioner, did their duty so thoroughly that much was spoken of their praise, at which service one Captain Bowsar and a valiant gentleman called Master MackWilliams were slain."

Bracamonte. Don Gonzalo de Bracamonte

This Spanish commander first came to the Netherlands in the army of the Duke of Alva. At that time he was in command of the Tercio de Sardinia, a formation of 1,600 men, a sixth of Alva's forces. He was a commander with a great reputation and remained in the Netherlands for a number of years. He was with the Spanish forces at both Heiligerlee and Jemmingen. After these engagements his regiment plundered and burned the countryside, and for this reason it was disbanded and the troops distributed among the other regiments (Famiano Strada, *History of the Low Country Wars*, VII, 57–58). In 1572 Bracamonte commanded a Flemish regiment at Ypres, and after the revolt of Holland (1572) he received orders to march from Ypres to 's Hertogenbosch, a shift of troops designed to make possible the relief of Middelburg. (See Johannes Brouwer, *Kronieken van Spaansche Soldaten uit het Begin van den tachtigjarigen Oorlog* [Zutphen, 1933], p. 176.)

Brandt. Marinus Brandt

A native of Saaftinge, and a famous Sea Beggar, Brandt took part in the capture of Brielle in 1572. On June 26, 1572 he conquered Gorkum and sent the clerics of that city to Brielle, where Lumey executed them. In the same year, under Bartel Entens, Brandt took part in the expedition against Goes, but the forces of the Prince of Orange were defeated by Mondragón. Also, in September of 1572, he repelled a fleet of ten Spanish ships bound for Goes. In 1573, when the Spanish were besieging Haarlem, Brandt was commander of the ships of the Prince of Orange on the Haarlemmermeer. His fleet suffered a severe defeat by the Spanish under Bossu. Brandt also took part in the siege of Middelburg in 1574 and was there taken prisoner by the Spanish. After obtaining his freedom, for some unexplained reason he went over to the Spanish side, and after that nothing was heard of him.

Brederode. Henry, Count of Brederode, Lord of Vianen (1531–1568)

Although his sister was married to a brother of Cardinal Granvelle, Brederode was one of the founders of the League of Nobles in 1565. He took the lead in the early years of the League, although his recklessness and lack of political talent did not fit him for the task. His opposition to the central government arose not so much from his being a convinced Protestant as from his profound dislike of the Catholic clergy and the small clique of advisers surrounding Margaret of Parma. On April 5, 1566, Brederode presented to Margaret of Parma the first petition of the Nobles protesting conditions in the Netherlands. This act gained him great popularity and thereafter he tried to persuade the high nobility to work with the League of Nobles. After the image-breaking he was one of the group who negotiated with Margaret of Parma and induced her to moderate the measures against Protestants.

When conditions in the Netherlands reached a state where it was necessary to choose between Philip of Spain and the rebels and Protestants, Brederode chose the latter. He was ready to use force to resist Philip II even before Orange saw that force would ultimately be necessary. He fortified his castle at Vianen and in February, 1567, entered into conversations with French Huguenot agents. In the same year he devised unsuccessful attacks on Walcheren, 's Hertogenbosch, and Utrecht. His efforts to gain control of Amsterdam were also unsuccessful. He fled to Germany and was declared banished by the government of the Netherlands. His own town of Vianen, where he had always allowed Protestantism to be practiced, was conquered by Meghen in 1568. He died at Reck-

Principal Persons Mentioned

linghausen in Westphalia February 15, 1568. (See M. C. van Hall, *Hendrik, Graaf van Brederode, Mede-grondlegger der Nederlandsche Vrijheid* [Amsterdam, 1844].)

Brederode. Lancelot van Brederode (died July 20, 1573)

A bastard son of Reinhoud III van Brederode, and a half brother of Hendrik van Brederode, Lancelot was one of the signers of the petition presented to Margaret of Parma in April, 1566, asking that the King abolish the Inquisition and the edicts against heresy. He had previously joined the League of Nobles. A great champion of Protestantism, Lancelot defended the preaching in open fields, many such services being held near his residence. He fled to Germany in 1567 but returned to the Netherlands and served under Ludwig of Nassau in the Battles of Heiligerlee and Jemmingen. Thereafter he obtained a privateering commission from the Prince of Orange and became one of the first of the Sea Beggars. Indeed, he was regarded by both friends and enemies as one of the most famous and daring of this group. He showed great courage at the taking of Brielle and later was a captain within Haarlem. When that city fell to the Spanish he was one of the captives beheaded by the victors, July 20, 1573.

Capres. Oudard, or Eduard Bournoville, or De Bournoville, Count of Hennin, Viscount of Barlin, Baron of Houllefort, Lord of Capres (1533–1585)

During the first campaign of Orange in Brabant in 1568, Capres served in the opposing forces and in 1572 was a colonel of a regiment of Walloons in the Spanish service. He served also under Don Fadrique at the siege of Haarlem. After the death of Requesens and the Pacification of Ghent, Capres was in command of a regiment for the States-General until 1578. In that year he joined with other disgruntled nobles, the faction known as the Malcontents, and aligned himself both against the States-General and the Calvinists. He was Governor of the city of Arras and was involved in Montigny's negotiations leading to the "Union of Arras" (January 6, 1579), a pact in which Hainaut, Artois, Rijssel, Douai, and Orchies united to maintain the Pacification of 1576. Capres was also active in bringing about a reconciliation between the Walloon provinces and the King. Orange, who deplored the Union of Arras, tried to win Capres over to his side, but Capres refused to accept the Prince's offers. He continued to serve Parma and Philip II and later received many honors from the Spanish crown.

Carleill. Christopher Carleill (1551–1593)

The son of a London vintner, Carleill was educated at Cambridge. He was at Flushing in 1572 and was present at the siege of Middelburg. He was held in high esteem by Boisot, the Dutch admiral. Carleill achieved a reputation as a brave commander, and the Prince of Orange placed him in charge of all the foreign soldiers in his camp. He served the Prince of Orange for five years and had a distinguished and varied career subsequent to his service in the Netherlands. He died in London, November 11, 1593. See the *D.N.B.*

Carlo, or Carloy, or Carloo. Gaspard van der Noot, Lord of Carloo (died 1573)

Carloo was a captain in the service of Philip II and had five hundred infantry under his command. At the time of the revolt he chose the side of William of Orange. He was a member of the League of Nobles and therefore fled in 1567 when Alva came to the Netherlands. He was accused before the Blood Council and banished *in absentia*. In April, 1568, he was involved in Groenendaal's attack on Alva and in the same year took part in the Prince of Orange's campaigns. In 1570 he was at Unico Manninga in East Friesland, and in 1572 he was a cavalry commander in the army sent by the Prince to relieve Haarlem. This force made a final effort to relieve the city in July, 1573, and Carloo perished in an action south of the city on July 8, 1573.

Chester. Edward Chester (died 1577)

Chester was the commander of a regiment of English mercenaries which arrived in the Netherlands in the spring of 1574. In the *Calendar of State Papers, Foreign, 1572–1574,* p. 473, under the date March 5, 1574, there are notes concerning a treaty with Spain. It appears that the Spanish were then already asking that Captain Chester and others serving Spain's rebellious subjects in Holland be commanded to return to England. Chester's regiment was dismissed as a regiment from States' service June 3, 1574, but a number of companies, including one commanded by Chester, remained in the service of the States of Holland until June, 1577.

In the *Calendar of State Papers, Foreign, 1573,* there are a number of letters by Chester to Burghley giving general news about the Netherlands and one letter from Chester to the Queen. In April, 1576, the Spanish flattered themselves that they could induce Chester to turn traitor. James Ferguson, *Scots Brigade in Holland* (Edinburgh, 1899), I, note pp. 10–11, quotes a letter from a Spanish agent in London to Secretary Zayas which says, "With regard to the matter of the plan of Flushing, I have had several conferences with Colonel Chester, the Englishman, and have agreed that he and Colonel Daburd of the Scotch forces will deliver the town of Flushing to His Majesty for 300,000 crowns and all the plunder that the soldiers can take." In spite of this communication, Chester remained true to the States of Holland and by resolution of the States of Holland August 18, 1577, was strongly recommended to the States-General as a regimental commander. He died shortly thereafter.

Chevraux, Henri de Vienne, Baron de Chevraux

This name is written by Williams "Baron Chiffero," but since in his list of commanders he omits Baron Chevraux, known to be present at the siege of Haarlem, and adds "Baron Chiffero," of whom there is no record, there seems little doubt that Chevraux is meant. This commander in the Spanish forces was a Burgundian nobleman and commanded Burgundian troops in the Netherlands for many years. In the *Calendar of State Papers, Foreign,* he is mentioned many times. In 1578 he was forced to break off his activities in the Netherlands because the French had entered Burgundy and seized his castle. Jacques Rossel, an English agent in the Low Countries, writing to Walsingham, October 12, 1578 (*Calendar of State Papers, Foreign, 1578–1579,* p. 235), says that the French incursion into Burgundy is more in the nature of marauding than war, and that Chevraux had hastened home with eight cornets of horse and eleven ensigns of Burgundian infantry.

Coligny. Gaspard de Châtillon, Count de Coligny (1519–1572)

A nephew of the influential Montmorency, Coligny made rapid

strides at the court of Henry II. In 1547 he was general of infantry; in 1555 Governor of Picardy. He was taken prisoner at the Battle of Saint-Quentin and remained a prisoner until 1559. Thereafter he was Governor of the Ile-de-France. He chose the side of Condé when Condé revolted against the royal power. He was a Calvinist and after 1562 the army commander of the Huguenots in the religious wars. He exercised a strong influence over Charles IX, whom he endeavored to persuade to become a Protestant. He wished to develop the French anti-Hapsburg policy to embrace a defense of Calvinism and to this end sought to bring about an alliance with William of Orange. He made bitter enemies of Catherine de' Medici and the Guises and was the first person murdered in the Massacre of St. Bartholomew, August 24, 1572.

Comines. Philippe de Comines (1445–1509)

This French historian and diplomat served first the Court of Burgundy and later the Kings of France. He wrote the highly valuable *Mémoires sur les règnes de Louis XI et de Charles VIII*, first printed in 1524 and 1528 and often reprinted thereafter.

Cornellys. Captain Cornellys (died 1577)

Le Petit, *La grande chronique*, II, 263, says, "There was also a Scot named Cornille who had previously been an ensign in Haarlem and, having escaped the hands of the Spanish, came to Alkmaar and did great things against the enemy." It would appear that "Cornille" is Le Petit's French rendition of Cornellys. Very few soldiers escaped from Haarlem, a handful of Scottish officers being the fortunate few. C. Ekama, *Beleg en Verdediging van Haarlem in 1572 en 1573* (Haarlem, 1872), p. 254, says, "Three days later [August 11, 1573] the Captain of the Scots [Balfour] was conveyed out of Haarlem and with six other persons concealed in the hospital. The following day the common Scottish soldiers to the number of 235 were beheaded. The Duke of Alva had previously ordered that not a single Walloon, Huguenot, or Englishman should be left alive." It appears almost certain, therefore, that Williams' Cornellys and Le Petit's "Cornille" are the same man. One last word on Cornellys should be added. In a letter of Davison to Walsingham, October 4, 1577 (*Calendar of State Papers, Foreign, 1577–1578*, p. 226), the writer, speaking of the forces be-

sieging Breda, says that "one Captain Cornellys, a Scot, attempting
to have made a trench hard under the wall on Monday night last,
was, with three or four of his company, slain under the walls."

Cressonière. Jacques de la Cressonière (died 1573)

Cressonière was Governor of the city of Gravelines. With his
help, Noircarmes, Stadholder of Hainaut and a loyal follower of
Philip II, was able to conquer Valenciennes after the turbulent
Calvinists had seized the government. In 1570 he commanded a
band of ordnance. He was an excellent engineering officer and was
especially skilled in siege methods. At the siege of Haarlem, as
Williams indicates, he was Great Master of the Artillery in the
army of Don Fadrique. He was killed early in 1573.

Donkus. Dorkus

The most reasonable explanation of this name is that Don Rodrigo de Toledo, Lord of Villorias and of Doncos is meant. Don
Rodrigo belonged to a cadet branch of the Duke of Alva's family
and was one of the principal commanders in the Netherlands. At
Haarlem he commanded the Tercio of Naples, and he was slain in
an assault on that city on the night of January 30, 1573. There was
also at Haarlem, in the Tercio of Lombardy, a captain named
Martin D'Orcaes. He was wounded January 30, 1573, and may be
the person Williams refers to, but since Williams is speaking only
of principal commanders, Don Rodrigo, Lord of Doncos, seems the
more likely person.

Drise

No reference has been found to a Captain Drise. The name may
be a typographical mangling of Captain Price, a well-known captain serving in the Netherlands.

Druynen. Godefroy von Haestricht, Lord of Druynen (died 1572)

Williams says that Druynen (which he spells Drume) was killed
when the forces of Orange attacked the Spanish trenches. Actually
he was killed in the surprise night attack by the Spanish on the
camp of William of Orange. In a letter to his brother, John of Nassau, September 21, 1572, the Prince says, "But since then they
[the Spanish] have regained their courage to the point where they
have delivered a surprise attack on us in which I have lost my
officer of justice of Breda, the Lord of Drunen, and the Italian cap-

Principal Persons Mentioned

tain Paul Camill, with several others" (Guillaume Groen van Prins-
terer, *Archives ou correspondance inédite de la maison d'Orange-
Nassau* [Leiden, 1835–1847], series I, vol. 3, p. 506).

**Egmond. Lamoraal, Count of Egmond, and Prince of Gavere (1522–
1568)**

Egmond was created Prince of Gavere in 1553. He possessed
extensive estates in Holland and Flanders. Entering the army at
an early age, he took part in the expedition of Charles V against
Tunis. He returned to the Netherlands in 1542. He enjoyed the
special favor of Charles V, who conferred a number of honorable
commissions on him. In 1552 he fought in Luxembourg and was
made governor of that province. Among other actions, he was at
the siege of Metz in 1552. In 1554 he took part in the negotiations
in England for the marriage of Philip II and Mary, and two years
later he saw service in the war against France, being commander
of the light cavalry. He played a large part in the victories of Saint-
Quentin and Gravelines. In 1559 he was Stadholder of Flanders
and Artois, a member of the Council of State, and commander of
the Spanish troops in the Netherlands. For a time, together with
Orange and Hoorne, he led the opposition to Granvelle, but he remained true to the Roman Catholic Church and loyal to Philip II.
He disapproved of the image-breaking and did not flee at Alva's
coming in 1567 as did many another. He was taken prisoner with
Hoorne and beheaded in 1568. He had great personal charm, yet
in a number of aspects was very naïve.

Eloy. Captain Eloy

Le Petit, *La grand chronique*, vol. II, mentions this captain a
number of times. He says (p. 228) that on August 25, 1572, all the
soldiers who were in Flushing embarked on an expedition against
Antwerp, with the exception of three or four companies, notably
those of Bernaert, Eloy, and Morgan. He mentions Eloy as commanding a company of Walloons in 1573 and adds (p. 258) that
on August 8, 1573, the Spanish forces having entrenched themselves near Haaks in Zeeland, the troops of Orange attacked them
and during the attack Eloy lost an eye.

**Entens. Jonker Barthold Entens van Mentheda tot Middelstum,
Dorema, and Engelboort (1539–1580)**

Principal Persons Mentioned

A rough, valiant, North Netherlands nobleman, Entens had lost a great part of his estates by riotous living. He joined the League of Nobles in 1566 and fled at the coming of Alva in 1567. He served in the army of Ludwig of Nassau at Heiligerlee and Jemmingen. In 1569 he became one of the Sea Beggars and from his base in East Frisia he plundered the Frisian Islands. In 1572 he operated from England and was then vice-admiral of the Sea Beggars. He served as Lumey's lieutenant at the capture of Brielle (April 1, 1572), and conquered Dort in the summer of 1572. His conduct gave rise to many complaints, and for this reason he was summoned to Delft in 1573 by the Prince of Orange and imprisoned. Obtaining his freedom, he invaded Friesland in 1576 and remained for a time in Groningen and Friesland. When in 1580 the city of Groningen had been betrayed to the Spanish, Entens was one of the besiegers of the city and was killed there.

Espernon. Jean Louis de Nogaret, de la Valette, duc d'Espernon (1554–1642)

Espernon was one of the favorites of Henry III of France. The King heaped honors on him at first, but when Espernon fell into disfavor, the King took back all that he had given. Espernon was at first an enemy of Henry IV, but later the two were reconciled, and Espernon was in the carriage with him when the King was assassinated. Espernon's career in France was turbulent, but he was outstanding neither as a soldier or a diplomat.

Fadrique. Don Fadrique de Toledo, Duke of Huesca (1529–1583)

The eldest son of the Duke of Alva and one of the foremost commanders for Philip II in the Netherlands, Don Fadrique was sent to the Netherlands in 1567. As commander of the infantry he took part in the campaign against William of Orange in 1568. In 1572 he defeated the troops of Genlis, which had been sent to relieve Mons, and he himself besieged Mons, which was in the hands of Ludwig of Nassau. After the fall of Mons, Alva and Don Fadrique conquered Malines. In the second half of 1572 and the beginning of 1573 Don Fadrique took Maastricht, Zutphen, Amersfoort, and Naarden. In Naarden and Zutphen his troops perpetrated horrible massacres. Following the actions mentioned he besieged Haarlem, a siege that endured from December, 1572, until July, 1573. He then attempted to take Alkmaar but was forced to raise the siege of that city on October 8, 1573. Shortly thereafter Alva and Don Fadrique left the Netherlands.

Fant. Anthony Fant (died 1574)

Apparently Fant continued to serve in the Netherlands until killed in the Battle of Mook, April 14, 1574. Thomas Churchyard, in *A Lamentable and Pitiful Description of the Woeful Wars in Flanders*, 1578 (STC 5239), pp. 53–54, says, "The Count Ludwig had done very great things in sundry enterprises and service of no little charge and hazard, . . . but the Duke did always so pursue him with a great power and great practices that he could not, nor was not able to, prevent the Duke's policies and stratagems. And so, at an overthrow which fell on the Count Ludwig's side, he was forced to fly and, as some affirm, was either drowned or slain after. Master Clap and Master Font, English gentlemen, were at this service and Font was slain there." He is not mentioned in Ten Raa and Bas, *Het Staatsche Leger*, the standard history of the Dutch army.

Fiennes. Jonker Gislain de Fiennes, Lord of Lumbres (died 1580)

Lumbres was a member of the League of Nobles and as a consequence was condemned by the Blood Council. Thereafter he adhered to the party of Orange and Ludwig of Nassau. In May, 1568, he was in England endeavoring to get help from the lowlands refugees there, a task in which he showed more industry than discretion. Subsequently he often represented Orange in England and France. In 1570 he was named admiral of the Sea Beggars, but he did not succeed in restraining those unruly seamen or in using them in important undertakings. He soon became involved in a quarrel with Lumey and was removed from his command. After the Peace of Saint-Germain he negotiated to have France take Orange under her protection. After 1571 he was also involved in negotiations in Germany. He died in 1580.

Frundsberg. Georg Frundsberg

The name is variously spelled Frundsberg, Fronsberg, or Frinsberg. This German nobleman was a colonel in a regiment of German mercenaries which was for many years in the service of Spain in the Netherlands. As Williams indicates, Frundsberg was present at the siege of Haarlem in 1573 and was one of the negotiators on the Spanish side for the surrender of the city on July 4, 1573. On the orders of Don John of Austria, he put his forces into Breda in 1577, but Hohenlohe, general of the forces of the State-General, besieged the city. The town was betrayed to Hohenlohe and Frundsberg was taken prisoner. In the *Calendar of State Papers, Foreign, 1577–1578,* p. 489, there is a letter from the Emperor to the Estates of the Low Countries expressing satisfaction that the Dutch have given Frundsberg his liberty. Earlier there had been other famous mercenaries with the name of Frundsberg. (See Pierre de Bourdeille, Seigneur de Brantôme, *Oeuvres complètes* [Paris, 1864–1882], I, 353.)

Genlis. Jean de Hangest, Seigneur de Genlis (died 1573)

Jean Hangest was the younger brother of François Hangest, Sieur de Genlis, a famous Protestant leader. After the death of François, Jean inherited his title of Seigneur de Genlis. He fought in the French religious wars and also in Flanders, being present at the capture of Valenciennes in 1570. As Williams indicates, he brought troops to the aid of Ludwig of Nassau at Mons, but his forces were attacked by those of Don Fadrique before he reached Mons; the French were defeated and Genlis was captured. He was imprisoned in the citadel of Antwerp and one morning in November, 1573, before Alva left the Low Countries, Genlis was found strangled in his bed.

Gilbert. Sir Humphrey Gilbert (1539–1583)

Both a soldier and a sailor, Gilbert served in Ireland before being sent to the Netherlands. He arrived in the Low Countries in 1572 in command of 1,500 English volunteers who had been engaged by Johan van Cuyck, Lord of Herpt, on the orders of the Prince of Orange. Although not sent officially by the English government, his instructions from the government were in effect that his primary objective was not to help the Dutch or fight the Spanish but to foil the French volunteers in their efforts to obtain advantage in the Low Countries.

After making an incursion into Flanders nearly to the gates of Bruges, Gilbert and his troops withdrew to Flushing. Gilbert twice besieged Goes unsuccessfully. On the second occasion he was obliged to raise the siege by Mondragón's famous march of ten miles across the drowned lands. The English fled before the well-disciplined Spanish infantry, and early in 1573 Gilbert returned to England in disgust. See the *D.N.B.*

Gourdan. Girault de Mauleon, Sieur de Gourdan

As Williams indicates, this nobleman was for many years Governor of Calais. In a letter to Queen Elizabeth's Secretaries, *Calendar of State Papers, Foreign, 1577–1578*, p. 712, Sir Amias Paulet says that Gourdan is known to be wholly on the side of the house of Guise.

Grand Prior. Fernando or Hernando de Toledo, Grand Prior of San Juan in Castile

The Grand Prior was a natural son of the Duke of Alva and came to the Netherlands with his father in 1567. He resided at first in Brussels, and on September 9, 1567, gave a famous banquet at which Egmond and Hoorne were guests. Following this banquet the two noblemen were seized, never to regain their freedom. The Grand Prior was a member of the Blood Council, but by avocation he was a cavalry commander. In 1568 he was ordered to prevent the Prince of Orange from recruiting troops in the Prince-Bishopric of Liège, where there were many rebels and refugee Huguenots. In July of the same year he took part in the campaign against Ludwig of Nassau, and at that time in addition to commanding cavalry he often commanded a great part of the infantry as well. Also, in the spring of 1568, he was with the forces opposing the Prince of Orange when he made his incursion into Brabant and Liège. He was at the capture of Maastricht by the Spanish troops, and in 1578 he commanded troops at the Battle of Gembloux, where the army of the States-General suffered a heavy defeat. He was also present at the Spanish defeat at Rymenam in 1578. Thereafter he returned to Spain and was one of the planners of the Invincible Armada. He was a serious but somewhat irritable man, a lover of art, and a collector of paintings.

Granvelle. Antoine Perrenot, Cardinal Granvelle (1517–1586)

Cardinal Granvelle was born in Besançon. He studied at the Universities of Paris, Padua, and Louvain and was initiated in 1538 into the affairs of government by his father, a trusted minister of Charles V. In that year he became Bishop of Arras. In 1550 Granvelle succeeded his father as Councilor, Great Chancellor, and Master of Requests for Charles V. He was very influential in domestic, international, and religious affairs during the latter years of that monarch. In 1559 Philip II appointed him to the Secret Council of Margaret of Parma, the Regent or Governess in the Netherlands. As presiding member of the Council of State, he supported vigorously the measures taken by Philip II against heretics, even though he did not agree with those measures in all details. He was also a sturdy supporter of the principle of a centralized state, but this fact was less an evidence of an adherence to Spanish absolutism than of inherited belief in the old Burgundian ideal of unity. The Compromise, or League of Nobles, was formed largely because of the antagonism existing between the nobles and Granvelle. The nobles pressed the King to recall him, and a number of them refused to attend the sessions of the Council of State because of his presence (1563). Within a few years Granvelle had managed to make himself the most hated man in the Netherlands. Eventually Philip II was forced to yield to pressure and in 1564 recalled him to Franche-Comté on a pretext. Granvelle had subsequently a distinguished career in the service of Spain. Despite his record in the Netherlands, he was a good administrator and a discerning patron of arts and letters.

Guise

A French ducal family, a younger branch of the family of the Dukes of Lorraine. Under Henry II, the Guises formed a powerful court party and in the reign of Francis II were the actual rulers of France. During the religious wars the Guises were the leaders of the Catholic Party. When, in 1584, the Protestant Henry of Navarre became successor to the throne, the Guises strengthened their bonds with Spain. Williams may refer to the family or to any one of the following:

François de Lorraine (1519–1563), second Duke of Guise, statesman and general. As has been indicated, he and his brother controlled the government under Francis II. The massacre of the Protestants at Vassy by his servants caused the outbreak of the wars of religion in France. He was assassinated in 1563.

Principal Persons Mentioned

Charles de Guise, Cardinal de Lorraine (1525–1574). A brother of the above, Charles developed power under Henry II and with his brother dominated the reign of Francis II. Learned, acute, subtle, princely of bearing, and a master of intrigue, he exercised great influence outside of France as well as within it. He was a bitter foe of the Huguenots and obtained from Philip II Spanish support for the Catholic cause in France. Of all the Guises he was probably the most able and most hated.

Henri de Lorraine, third Duke of Guise (1550–1588). Henri was the oldest son of François, the second Duke of Guise, and thus was a nephew of the Cardinal of Lorraine. Henri's chief claim to infamy is his cooperation with Catherine de' Medici in planning the Massacre of St. Bartholomew. In 1576 he formed the Catholic League and enjoyed wide popularity in all classes of society. He overshadowed King Henry III, who cooperated with him but who finally arranged his assassination.

Louis de Lorraine, Cardinal de Guise (1555–1588). Louis, a brother of the third Duke, was killed about the same time as his brother.

Hasselaar. Kenau S. Hasselaar (1526–1588 or 1589)

Kenau Hasselaar was born in Haarlem of a well-to-do family and married Nanning Gerbrandszoon Borst, a shipbuilder, by whom she had four children. By 1571 she was a widow. After her husband's death, she carried on a timber business and, as is indicated here, achieved fame during the siege of her native city, but not as the captain of a company of Amazons. Apparently she was a brave businesswoman who did all that she could during the siege to aid in the city's defense. She encouraged the defenders, carried ammunition, worked to repair the walls, and contributed money for the defense. A contemporary says that she went about armed with a pistol and short spear, but she was not the vixen which legend has sometimes made of her. See J. W. Wijn, *Het Beleg van Haarlem,* pp. 52–53, and Gerda H. Kurtz, *Kenu Symonsdochter van Haarlem* (Assen, 1956).

Hasselaar. Pieter Dirks Hasselaar (ca. 1555–ca. 1616)

Williams spells this name Ashilers, but it seems probable that he meant Hasselaar. Both Ekama, *Beleg . . . van Haarlem,* p.

Principal Persons Mentioned

192, and A. J. van der Aa, *Biographisch Woordenboek* (Haarlem, 1852–1878), indicate that Hasselaar was at Kaag with the fleet of the States and the Prince of Orange. Hasselaar was a prominent figure in the siege of Haarlem and later was well known as a seaman and merchant.

Haultain. Alexander de Zoete de Lake, called Haultain (died 1585)
Haultain was Lieutenant Governor of Flushing when Tseraerts was Governor there. Both Haultain and Tseraerts arrived at Haarlem on April 18, 1573, and Haultain left the city on June 17, 1573. In the same year he was appointed commander of the life guards of the Prince of Orange (Ten Raa and Bas, *Het Staatsche Leger*, I, 120). On August 31, 1573, he was Governor of Walcheren (Ten Raa and Bas, I, 222). He was at the same time chief of troops in Zeeland. In 1580 he gave up his functions as captain of the guard of the Prince.

Havré. Charles Philippe de Croy, Marquis of Havré (1549–1613)
In 1568, at the age of nineteen, Croy began his military career in the service of Spain. When, in 1574, Requesens raised fifty-five companies of Walloon infantry, he gave Croy command of twenty of them. Actually Croy was raised to a marquisate in 1575 and in that year he went to Spain both to represent Requesens and to thank the King for his new title. He was held in Spain under a variety of pretexts but returned to the Netherlands in August, 1576. In the same year Havré endeavored to patch up the long-existing quarrel between the Croys and the Nassaus. He was at Antwerp during the Spanish Fury and only saved himself by fleeing to the ships of the Prince of Orange. He was one of the high nobility who in 1576 negotiated to bring Archduke Matthias to the Netherlands as Viceroy in order to lessen the power of Orange. In January, 1578, when the finances of Holland and Zeeland were in a very bad state and war taxes pressed heavily, he was sent by the States-General to England to obtain help. It was through the mediation of Havré that on January 7, 1578, Elizabeth agreed, among other things, to place five thousand infantry and one thousand cavalry at the disposal of the Prince, subject to certain conditions. About 1580, in the time of the "treason" of Rennenberg, Havré also went over to the side of Philip II. He was later em-

ployed by the King on diplomatic missions and was a member of the Council of State and chief of finances. He was created a Knight of the Golden Fleece in 1599 and died in 1613.

Hohenlohe. Wolfgang, Count of Hohenlohe

Wolfgang was a brother-in-law of the Prince of Orange, having married Magdalena von Nassau, a younger sister of the Prince. His brother Philip, Count of Hohenlohe, was also on the side of Orange and acquired greater prestige than did Wolfgang. Williams spells the name "Holdestocke" and "Holhocke," but such spellings of this name by Englishmen were not unusual at the time.

Hoorne. Philip of Montmorency-Nivelle, Count of Hoorne (1518–1568)

Hoorne was a rich and important Netherlandish nobleman. In 1546 he was at the court of Charles V. In 1549 he accompanied Philip II on his journey to Germany and the Netherlands, and in 1556 he was made a Knight of the Golden Fleece. He fought against France in the Battle of Saint-Quentin. He was Stadholder of Gelderland and after that Admiral of the Netherlands. In 1559 he had command of the fleet that took Philip II to the Netherlands. In 1561 he returned to the Netherlands and was a member of the Council of State. Together with Orange and Egmond he worked for the removal of Granvelle and for more influence for the Netherlands nobles in the government of the country. Although a good Catholic, he was tolerant of the reformed religion. He remained true to the central government and paid his respects to Alva when the Duke came to the Netherlands in 1567. Hoorne was taken prisoner by Alva, accused of high treason, and beheaded in the Great Market at Brussels on June 5, 1568.

Johan, or John IV, Count of Nassau-Dillenburg-Katzenellenbogen (1535–1606)

Usually known in Dutch history as Jan or John of Nassau, he was the second son of William the Rich and Juliana von Stolberg. He was brought up at Dillenburg and inherited the greater part of the Nassau property. In 1568 and 1572 he supported his brother William of Orange in his campaigns in the Netherlands, the plans for which were prepared at Dillenburg. The campaign of Ludwig of Nassau in 1574 was also prepared in collaboration with John and he supported his brother Ludwig financially. He had turned to Calvinism in 1572 and after that devoted himself solely to the affairs of the revolt. In 1577 he was appointed Stadholder of Gelderland by Archduke Matthias, who had been named Viceroy. As Stadholder he worked with the able chancellor Leoninus and stoutly upheld Calvinism in Gelderland against much opposition. For a number of reasons, among them the death of his wife, the continued opposition of the Catholics in Gelderland, and the success of Parma's armies, he returned to Nassau in July, 1580. He did not go back to the Netherlands, although he continued to support his brother. His last years were largely occupied with efforts to recover the great sums which he and his brothers had advanced to the States-General. In this endeavor he had some success. He also worked to bring about cooperation between the Protestant German princes and the States-General, but in these efforts he was unsuccessful.

Don John of Austria (1547–1578)

Don John was the bastard son of Charles V by Barbara Blomberg. His first notable action was the suppression of the revolt of the Moors in Granada in 1570. As is well known, he commanded at the Battle of Lepanto, and that victory over the Turks was his greatest feat. In 1576, he was appointed Viceroy of the Netherlands but arrived there at an inauspicious moment, when the whole country was momentarily united against the Spanish. He was forced to accept the Pacification of Ghent and he agreed to withdraw the Spanish troops from the Netherlands. Finding himself powerless without troops, he reversed his attitude. On July 24, 1577, he seized the citadel of Namur, recalled the Spanish troops, and thus began a return to power. He gained an important victory over the Netherlanders at Gembloux, but he died not long afterward. He was succeeded by Parma.

Kenau. See Hasselaar

La Motte. Valentin de Pardieu, Lord de la Motte (1530–1595)

La Motte chose the side of the Spanish in the troubles in the Low Countries. He took part in the Battle of Austruweel, March 13, 1567, and served bravely with the Spanish army besieging Mons (1572), where he was lieutenant of the Spanish artillery. He fought and was wounded at the siege of Haarlem (1573). As a reward for his bravery he was made Governor of Gravelingen (1574). Later he signed the Union of Brussels and became an officer in the army of the States-General. He strongly disliked Calvinists and soon became discontented. He was instrumental in the formation of the group called the "Malcontents," and when eventually he became reconciled to the Spanish crown he was a leader in bringing over other Malcontents to the Spanish side. He fought bravely for Parma and was wounded on two occasions subsequent to the wound received at Haarlem. He conquered Dunkirk (1583), took part in the campaign in France (1590–1592), and occupied Nijmegen with Parma (1591). Between 1592 and 1595 he fought in Groningen, conquered Hoei, and subsequently served in France, where he was killed by a musket shot at Doullens. On one occasion the English plotted to get possession of both Gravelines and La Motte by treason, but the plot was discovered by Bernardino de Mendoza.

La Noue. François de la Noue (1541–1591)

La Noue was well known both as a soldier and as a writer. He became a Huguenot in 1558. He was already a veteran soldier when he entered the Netherlands, having served in Italy, in the religious wars in France, and against the Spanish. In 1570 he received a wound which necessitated the amputation of his left arm; an artificial arm was then contrived for him which permitted him to hold the reins of his horse. He was thereafter known as "Bras de fer."

As Roger Williams indicates, he was with Ludwig of Nassau in his campaign in Hainaut in 1572. He captured Valenciennes at the end of May of that year and was in Mons when that city was besieged by Alva. When the city capitulated, he was released on his promise not to serve against Spain for a year. After various adventures in France, he returned and served the States-General in 1578–1580. In 1580 he was taken prisoner by Parma and remained a prisoner until 1585. Subsequently he fought in the wars of religion in France. Williams several times says that he learned much about the art of war from François de la Noue. He wrote *Discours politiques et militaires* (Basle, 1587), and a number of other works have been attributed to him. The literature on La Noue is voluminous.

La Rivière. Captain la Rivière

Le Petit, *La grande chronique,* p. 228, says that Captain la Rivière was killed in Zeeland in 1572 and that this so infuriated his Huguenot soldiers that they killed all their prisoners. Since Williams indicates that his Captain la Rivière was also in command of Huguenot troops in Zeeland in 1572, it seems probable that the same person is meant. Eugene Haag, *La France Protestante* (Paris, 1846–1859), cautions that there were a number of Huguenot leaders named La Rivière and that it is not always possible to know which one is meant.

Le Duc. Ambroise le Duc

Williams speaks of Le Duc as a Walloon rebel who in 1572 made his way north to Zeeland to join the forces of the Prince of Orange. With other commanders he defended the city of Flushing and was also present at the attempts to conquer Goes. In a letter to Secretary Walsingham, dated from Flushing, August 25, 1585, *Calendar of State Papers, Foreign, 1584–1585,* p. 679, Roger Williams says that he has talked to a number of men of good judgment and experience, among them Ambroise Duke, and all agreed that the Spanish intended to invade England. This letter, together with what is said of Le Duc in the present volume, indicates that Williams and Le Duc were probably friends and companions for many years. Le Duc is also mentioned by Le Petit, *La grande chronique,* who says on page 249 that Le Duc was wounded in an attempt upon the city of Tolen in 1572, and again, on page 267, that Le Duc was wounded outside Middelburg in 1573.

Licques. Philip de Recourt, Baron of Licques

This commander was at the siege of Haarlem (1573) and in 1578, together with Montigny, was one of the leaders of the "Malcontents." In 1580 he was apparently Governor of Louvain, and following this he was for a time (about 1581) Governor of Doornik.

Lorges. Jacques de Montgomery, Comte de Lorges, and later Comte de Montgomery

As Williams indicates, Lorges was the eldest son of Gabriel de

Principal Persons Mentioned

Montgomery, Comte de Montgomery, the famous Huguenot leader who while captain of the guard wounded Henry II's eye in a tournament. The wound was the cause of the French king's death. The son was also a well-known Huguenot leader, but he never attained the fame of his father. In 1573 he led French and English troops to assist Batenburg, who was attempting to relieve Haarlem.

Lovell. Thomas Lovell

In a letter written from The Hague to Walsingham, September 30/October 10, 1584 (*Calendar of State Papers, Foreign, 1584–1585*, p. 83), Lovell says, "I have known and borne offices in these countries for twelve years." This statement would place him in the first English companies to arrive in the Netherlands. In a later letter to Walsingham, October 14/24, 1585 (*Calendar of State Papers, Foreign, 1585–1586*, p. 86), Lovell says, "It is well known that I have served long in these countries and have borne divers offices as sergeant, ancient-bearer [i.e., standard-bearer] and lieutenant. Afterwards the Prince and the States of Holland preferred me to be lieutenant of the ordnance, and when the force of the enemy was so strong that we could not longer be in the field but were driven to keep our towns, and so it was needless to hold any in that office, they gave me a commission to be sergeant major of Colonel William Thorpe's regiment, which I discharged for two years. Then, having much to do in law matters, I sought my discharge, and after this the State made me commissary and muster-master of their soldiers in Holland, where I have employed myself till now." Ten Raa and Bas, I, 213, note that Thomas Lonel (*sic*) is the sergeant major of the regiment commanded by Jonkheer Willem van Dorp, the commander designated by Lovell as William Thorpe.

Ludwig, or Lodewijk, or Louis, of Nassau (1538–1574)

Ludwig was one of the four younger brothers of William the Silent and the brother who played the largest part in the affairs of William and the revolt of the Netherlands. He was an energetic Protestant and is considered by some to have been a good soldier. In 1557–1558 he fought on the Spanish side against the French. Ludwig was a member of the League of Nobles from its beginning.

Principal Persons Mentioned

In 1567 he fled to Germany, where in 1568 he was commander of the army that made an incursion into Friesland and Groningen. He won the Battle of Heiligerlee but was defeated at Jemmingen. In 1569 he was in France, where he sought to obtain the support of the Huguenots for the revolt in the Netherlands. He had been a Lutheran but became a Calvinist at La Rochelle. With a small army which was gathered with the support of the French king, he surprised and captured Mons in Hainaut in 1572 but lost the city again in September. In 1574, again with the help of France, he gathered an army of thirteen thousand, which was disastrously defeated by Sancho de Avila at Mook on April 14, a battle in which both he and his brothers Henry and Christopher lost their lives. An account of the Battle of Mook is given by Sir Charles W. C. Oman, *A History of the Art of War in the Sixteenth Century* (London, 1937).

For the activities of Ludwig in France, see Pieter J. van Herwerden, *Het Verblijf van Lodewijk van Nassau in Frankrijk* (Assen, 1932).

Lumbres. See Fiennes

Lumey. Willem van der Marck, Lord of Lumey, Count of the Empire (ca. 1542–1578)

Lumey was a South Netherlands nobleman. As a young man he plundered the region of Liège and stirred the Liègois into revolt against the Bishop (1566). His inclination to the reformed religion and his hatred of the Catholic clergy were exhibited as early as this time. He signed the Compromise or League of Nobles and was forced to flee in 1567. Sentence of banishment was pronounced against him in 1569. He joined the army of the Prince of Orange and commanded a troop of cavalry in 1568. After the failure of the forces of Orange in 1568, Lumey fled to Emden. In that port he fitted out privateers and joined the Sea Beggars, becoming admiral of the Beggars as successor to Fiennes. After the capture of Brielle, he became the Prince of Orange's commander in Zeeland. Later he was commandant of Holland and Zeeland, where he undertook several campaigns and showed himself extremely cruel to the Catholic clergy. Both an attack on Amsterdam and an attempt to relieve Haarlem were unsuccessful.

Principal Persons Mentioned

When he murdered Father Musius, the host of William of Orange at Delft, he was relieved of his offices and arrested. After obtaining his freedom, he went to Aachen. He later fought in the army of the States. He died at Liège, either from poison or from the bite of a mad dog (1578).

MacWilliams. See Bouser

Maisonfleur. Lhuillier, Seigneur de la Maisonfleur

In a letter to Queen Elizabeth, April 9, 1573 (*Calendar of State Papers, Foreign, 1572–1574*, pp. 307–308), Maisonfleur gives a long account of himself. He says that he served under the late Duc de Guise in Italy and that he was much esteemed by the Queen Mother. He admits that during the first religious troubles in France he had a command under the Duc de Guise and fought on the King's side, but then he had no more knowledge of the Gospel than St. Paul had before his conversion. Since, however, he has been called to a knowledge of religion, although the King and his mother have employed both prayers and menaces, he has not borne arms for them. On this account the Cardinal of Lorraine and the house of Guise have so hated him that during the last troubles they sent a provost marshal and thirty harquebusiers, who took him prisoner, although he was sick of a fever. For eight days on this occasion he was in danger of losing his head, for a charge was brought against him of having had preaching in his house, contrary to the edicts of the King. Everyone knows also that during the last massacre his house was pillaged. He confesses that until two or three months after the late massacre (St. Bartholomew) he did not think it lawful to take arms against the King; but, after hearing the arguments of certain ministers, he resolved to set out for La Rochelle and was detained only by the express commandment of the Duc d'Alençon. As for the lack of reformation that was observed in him whilst he was living at the court, he admits that he did not always live as chastely as he might, but there is no place so dangerous for a man disposed to gallantry as the court.

There is also much information on Maisonfleur in Conyers Read's biographies of Walsingham and Burghley.

Mandelsloo. Count Ernst von Mandelsloo

Principal Persons Mentioned

This German general was a high commander in the army of the Prince of Orange. He accompanied the Prince of Orange on his campaign in the South Netherlands in 1568. Bor, a famous Dutch historian, says that he resigned from the army of the Prince because the States-General was too parsimonious, his troops often being unpaid. After 1573 he took service under the French king. At the time of the death of the Prince of Orange he was still owed by the States-General for his service under Orange.

Mansfeld. Karel, Count van Mansfeld (1547–1596)

Karel was the son of Pieter Ernst van Mansfeld. Like his father, he first sided with the nobles, then became a supporter of the Regent, Margaret of Parma. Having killed the Provost of Yvoy in 1567, he fled to France and only succeeded in returning to the country in 1576. Thereafter he served under both John of Austria and Parma. In 1579 he followed Berlaymont as chief of the artillery. He engaged in many actions, including the siege of Antwerp (1583). After the death of Parma he was for a time commander of the Spanish armies. Subsequent to his service in the Low Countries, he held a command in the armies of the Emperor in Hungary and fought successfully against the Turks. He was killed at Gran.

Mansfeld. Pieter Ernst, Count van Mansfeld (1517–1604)

Mansfeld first saw service in the expedition of Charles V against Tunis. In 1543 he commanded a squadron of cavalry as a lieutenant of Reinhoud van Brederode, whose sister he married in 1546. In the war in Lorraine he was taken prisoner by the French and did not regain his freedom until 1557 in time to take part in the Battle of Saint-Quentin. In 1562 he took the side of Orange, Egmond, and Hoorne in their controversies with Margaret of Parma, but by 1565 he was firmly on the side of Spain and the central government. In 1569 he was placed by Alva in command of troops fighting the Huguenots in France and thereafter was named Governor of Luxembourg. In 1575 Requesens named him to the Council of State. After the death of Requesens, he commanded Netherlands troops, but his history made him suspect and he was imprisoned until March, 1577. Don John of Austria again gave him command of Spanish troops and he served under Don John and Parma. When Parma was absent for a time campaigning in France, Mansfeld served in his place as Governor General and later served for a time as Viceroy.

Marck. See Lumey

Marnix. See Saint Aldegonde

Meghen. Charles de Brimeu, Count of Meghen (1525–1572)

Meghen belonged to the important Flemish family of Humbercourt and was prominent in the Netherlands from early manhood. In 1554 he commanded fifteen companies of infantry. In 1556 he was made a Knight of the Golden Fleece and became Stadholder of Luxembourg. Two years later he exchanged this stadholdership for that of Hainaut, and in 1560 he followed Hoorne as Stadholder of Gelderland. As a stadholder he played an important role in the troubles in the Low Countries. At first, in company with all the other stadholders, he was opposed to the new bishoprics and joined in the fight against Granvelle when the nobles met at Hoogstraten. When at that meeting there was talk of violent opposition to the Spanish government, he parted company from his fellow nobles and from that time on was a loyal supporter of the Spanish crown. In 1566 and 1567 he endeavored to stamp out in his province the epidemic of desecration of Catholic churches and endeavored also to suppress the Calvinist preachers.

In 1567 he occupied with his troops the cities of 's Hertogenbosch, Vianen, Amsterdam, and Utrecht and thus prevented those favoring the Prince of Orange from seizing those places. At the Battle of Heiligerlee he arrived too late to save his friend Arenberg, but he did throw a garrison into Groningen and thus prevented Ludwig of Nassau from occupying the city. After Arenberg's death Meghen was Stadholder of Groningen, Friesland, and Overijssel.

He was both a proven military commander and an efficient civil administrator but was far from being an admirable man.

Mendoza. Juan de Mendoza

Bernardino de Mendoza says (*Commentaires de Bernardino de Mendoza* [Brussels, 1860], I, 286) that Philip II sent Juan de Mendoza to the Low Countries to join the troops besieging Mons as commander in chief of the light cavalry. Don Bernardino adds that Don Juan was a brother of the Lord of Salvatierra and was

Principal Persons Mentioned

prominent at the Spanish court. Don Bernardino de Mendoza was also present at the siege of Haarlem, although he is not the man mentioned by Williams.

Mondragón. Cristóbal Mondragón (1504–1596)

This Spanish general came to the Netherlands with Alva in 1567. He gave evidence many times of his courage and talent. He was Governor of Zeeland and was in command at Middelburg when that city was besieged for about a year (1573–1574) by the Sea Beggars. When the forces of Orange finally captured the city, it was agreed by the terms of the capitulation (February 21, 1574) that Mondragón and his troops were to leave Walcheren. Mondragón subsequently did valiant service for the Spanish and was highly respected by his enemies. In 1595, when he was ninety-one years old, he forced Prince Maurits to break the siege of Grol and defeated the troops of Philip of Nassau.

His most spectacular feat, and indeed one of the most remarkable in military history, was his march through the drowned lands in October, 1572. The sea had at one time broken the dikes of Beveland and flooded the villages and farm lands. These drowned lands separated Beveland from Brabant, but if one knew the way it was possible to pass through the water at low tide from Brabant to Beveland. Guided by natives familiar with the country, Mondragón led three thousand men through the water from Tholen (easily reached from Brabant) to Yerseke. The march was made at night. The water was never lower than the breasts of the men and sometimes above their shoulders. The expedition crossed ten miles of water in about five hours. By this march Goes was relieved and Middelburg also was saved for the time being. This feat was accomplished by Mondragón when he was sixty-eight years old. (See Ten Raa and Bas, I, 31.)

Monte. Juan Bautista del Monte

Del Monte was a cavalry captain much renowned for his bravery. He was prominent at the siege of Haarlem, where he defeated the forces of Batenburg, who had been sent by the Prince of Orange to relieve the city. He played an important part in the Spanish victory at Mook (1574), and later he was at the siege of

Principal Persons Mentioned

Antwerp. He had also an important part in the victory of Don John at Gembloux.

Montgomery. See Lorges

Morgan. Sir Thomas Morgan (died 1595)

In April, 1572, Morgan was appointed captain of the first band of English volunteers that served in the Low Countries under William of Orange. He landed at Flushing on June 6 of that year with a company of three hundred men. When Sir Humphrey Gilbert returned to England, Morgan returned also; but in February, 1573, Morgan again landed in the Low Countries, this time with ten English companies. He took part in the vain attempt to relieve Haarlem and in the fight before Middelburg. Owing to a disagreement regarding the payment of his troops, he returned to England early in January of 1574. He then served for a period in Ireland, but in 1578 he again volunteered for service in the Low Countries under Captain, afterward Sir John, Norris and took part in numerous battles in that year and the following years. He returned to England in 1584 but was back in the Netherlands a few months later. He was still in the Netherlands in 1593 as Governor of Bergen-op-Zoom. He died in England in 1595. See the *D.N.B.*

Morgan. Captain Walter Morgan

In Charles Oman's *Art of War in the Sixteenth Century*, p. 560, the author says, "In All Souls Library we have a marvellous series of contemporary sketches by Walter Morgan, one of Orange's English followers, who presented to Lord Burleigh a couple of dozen of his drawings, illustrating all campaigns from Orange's invasion of Brabant down to the end of 1573, including the sieges of Mons and Haarlem, and much naval fighting." Oman described the manuscript in an article in the *Archaeological Journal* and it was used by A. L. Rowse, *The Expansion of Elizabethan England* (London, 1955), pp. 344–345.

Morgan. Sir William Morgan (died 1584)

Morgan began his military career as a volunteer in France in the army of the Huguenots during the French religious wars. He later enlisted in the forces of Count Ludwig of Nassau, taking part in the capture of Valenciennes on May 24, 1572, and of Mons the following day. He left the Netherlands in 1573 and never returned. See the *D.N.B*

Morris, Captain

In the *Calendar of State Papers* there are a number of references to Captain Morris, but there may actually have been more than one captain by that name in the Netherlands. In the *Calendar of State Papers, Foreign, 1581–1582*, p. 401, there is a letter from Stokes to Walsingham, December 14, 1581, in which the writer notes that "The Prince [of Orange] has sent to this town [Bruges] five companies of English: 'to say,' Captain Cromwell, Captain Piggott, Captain Welshe, Captain Morris, and Captain Edwards." This letter seems to refer to the Morris whom Williams knew. Almost certainly, the present Captain Morris is the one referred to in William Blandy, *The Castle* (1581), f. 26 recto, where the author says that Captain Morris was "a man of great experience and knowledge in feats of war."

Mouy. Isaac de Vaudrey, Seigneur de Mouy

This soldier had a long and valuable career both in the Netherlands and in the French religious wars. He was overshadowed by his father, the distinguished Huguenot captain, Louis de Vaudrey, Seigneur de Mouy.

Muxica. Don Antonio de Muxica

This Spanish commander was killed the night of the camisado at Mons. He had seen many years of service in the Spanish army.

Orange. Prince William of Orange, or William the Silent (1533–1584)

The leader of the revolt against Spain in the Netherlands, William was murdered in 1584. There are numerous biographies of him, and biographical sketches may be found in the standard encyclopedias and biographical dictionaries. A good summary of his life is that given in the Columbia one-volume encyclopedia.

Pacheco. Isidoro Pacheco

Isidoro Pacheco was Governor of Goes. He was killed by a spear-thrust during the conquest of Duiveland in 1576. There was also in Alva's army in 1567 a Francisco Pacieco; and there was a Juan Pacheco who was a commander of Spanish infantry before Haarlem, 1572–1573.

Principal Persons Mentioned

Pacheco. Pedro Alvarez Pacheco

Pacheco, a relative of the Duke of Alva, arrived in the Netherlands in 1567 as colonel of a regiment. He took part in the campaign against Orange in 1568 and was Governor of Deventer in 1570. In 1572 Alva appointed him commander of the Spanish garrison in Flushing. Both Alva and Pacheco were ignorant of the fact that Flushing had fallen and was occupied by the Sea Beggars. When Pacheco arrived in the city, he was immediately taken prisoner by De Rijk. After a short trial he was condemned to death and hanged because of his cruelty during his term as Governor of Deventer.

Parma. Margaret, Duchess of Parma (1522–1586)

A natural daughter of the Emperor Charles V, Margaret was married in 1536, when she was fourteen, to Alessandro de' Medici, who died the following year. In 1538 she married Ottavio Farnese, later Duke of Parma. In 1559 she was named Regent of the Netherlands by her half brother, Philip II, and continued in that office until 1567. Some of her characteristics are widely known: that she had a moustache; that she was energetic and mannish and fond of riding and hunting; and that she suffered from gout. These unimportant bits of information have obscured the fact that she governed a turbulent province in a most difficult period, and that probably, considering all the circumstances, she did as well as anyone could have done. She later returned to the Netherlands when her son, Alessandro Farnese, Duke of Parma, was military commander there.

Pelham. Sir William Pelham (died 1587)

Pelham was a famous and irascible English soldier and at one time lieutenant general of the ordnance. He had a reputation as an expert in military matters. He was on a diplomatic mission in the Netherlands, briefly, in 1578, and returned with Leicester in 1586 to the Netherlands, where he was a resolute and useful commander. See the D.N.B

Polwiller. Baron Nicolas Polwiller

This German nobleman was for many years a commander of German mercenaries in the Netherlands on the side of Spain. In 1578 the States-General sought to have the Emperor compel

Principal Persons Mentioned

Polwiller to withdraw from the Netherlands. The *Calendar of State Papers, Foreign,* for the years 1576–1583, contains many notices of the colonel and his troops.

He was a commander at the siege of Haarlem and some years later commandant of the garrison at Roermond. In the same year (1578) he surrendered Deventer to Rennenberg. When in 1580 Parma reorganized his army, the regiment of Polwiller was discharged.

Poyet, Captain

Poyet was a Huguenot who distinguished himself in the first religious war in France. He was also a commander noted for his bravery in the second religious war. At the conclusion of that conflict he fought in the Low Countries under Ludwig of Nassau, as is indicated in Williams' narrative. He was Governor of Mons for a short time. Another Huguenot captain was named Payet, and the two, Poyet and Payet, are very often confused.

Reade. Sir William Reade

William Reade was knighted by Leicester (*Calendar of State Papers, Foreign, 1586–1587,* p. 214). Leicester had a high regard for Reade. "He [Sir William Stanley] and old Reade," Leicester wrote, "are worth their weight in pearls. They be two as rare captains as any prince living hath" (Leicester's *Correspondence,* p. 417). In a later letter to Walsingham, he said, "I assure you I never knew a worthier old fellow than old Reade is, nor so able [a] body to take pains; he hath passed all men here for pains and peril" (*Correspondence,* p. 30). In 1586 Sir John Norris wrote to Burghley to complain that Leicester had given the post of sergeant major, formerly filled by Captain Price, to Sir William Reade. Thomas Churchyard, *A General Rehearsal of Wars,* f. G1 verso, says of Reade that he was "a man so worthy of memory, and garnished with knowledge and courage, that he not only merits to be spoken of but likewise deserveth to be honored in martial causes and exercises of war."

Requesens y Zuñiga. Luis de Requesens y Zuñiga (1528–1576)

Requesens succeeded Alva as Governor of the Netherlands in 1573. Where Alva had sought to secure submission of the people by cruelty and terror, Requesens tried compromise and reason. He twice tried to negotiate peace with William of Orange. During his regime occurred the terrible and unsuccessful siege of Leiden by a Spanish army. Requesens, like other Spanish commanders, was plagued by the problem of unpaid and mutinous troops. He died suddenly and was succeeded as Governor by his former commander at Lepanto, Don John of Austria.

Robinson, or Robson

In the *Calendar of State Papers, Foreign, 1572–1574*, p. 365, June 6, 1573, it is indicated that "Captain Thomas Robson, having obtained license to levy three hundred waged men of war, [was] to depart to the Low Countries for serving against the persecutors of God's religion." On page 396 of the same volume, August 1, 1573, Captain Cockburn to H. Killegrew, the writer indicates that "he has heard of Captain Robson's great success; there is great number to follow, and embarking daily." On page 531, July 18, 1574, Killegrew to Walsingham, the writer says that "Captains Robinson and Adamson's companies are defeated in Holland and the Prince in great strait." It is not certain, of course, that Williams' "valiant Robinson, a Scottish captain" is the Thomas Robson or Robinson indicated here, but it appears probable.

Robles. Caspar de Robles, Lord of Billy (1527–1585)

Robles entered military service at an early age and speedily distinguished himself as a brave and capable soldier. In the Netherlands before the disturbances began he served for a time under the Prince of Orange. In the winter of 1566–1567 he took an important part in the suppression of the religious insurrections and was at the Battle of Jemmingen. In 1572 and 1573, in Friesland, he fought the forces of Orange with energy and success and kept Friesland loyal to Spain. Shortly after the Pacification of Ghent, Robles was for a time prisoner of the States-General. Upon regaining his freedom he joined Don John of Austria and was at the Battle of Gembloux. He later served under Parma. He was Stadholder of Friesland in 1573.

During his sojourn in Friesland he turned his attention to the control of the sea and the rivers (the ever-present problem in the

Netherlands) and in this peaceful pursuit had good success. He was killed by the explosion of the *kruitschip "van Giannibelli"* in 1585.

Roeulx or Roeux. Jean de Croy, Count of Roeulx (died 1581)

The Count was the son of Adrien de Croy. He was Governor at Tournai in 1567. Later he had the command of the same band of ordnance that his father had led. In 1576 he was Stadholder of Flanders and commander in chief of the troops of that province.

Rollé. Jeronimus de Rollé (died 1573)

Rollé was a member of an old South Netherlands family, although his estates were in Zeeland. In 1572 he supported the Prince, who named him a member of the Council of Zeeland. In August of that year Rollé made an unsuccessful attempt to persuade the government of the city of Zierikzee to go over to the side of the Prince and the States-General. In the troublesome days that followed, he distinguished himself by his fearlessness and resolution. He gave orders that his castle of West Souberg should be burned rather than that it should be used by the Spanish as a base from which to oppress Vlissingen. Shortly thereafter he devised a plan to capture Tholen. In the furious fight to carry out the plan in May, 1573, Rollé and a number of other valuable commanders were killed, and Tholen remained in the hands of the Spanish.

Romero. Julián Romero (died 1578)

When Philip II decided in 1559 to keep the Spanish troops in the Low Countries, Romero was one of two Spanish commanders ranking immediately below Orange and Egmond. In 1567 he was commander of the Tercio of Sicily. He was a commander of troops in the Spanish force which captured Naarden in 1572, and he inflicted cruelty and death on great numbers of the inhabitants of that city. He fought against Count Ludwig at Jemmingen. Later he conquered Spaarndam and lost an eye at the siege of Haarlem. He was also present at the capture of Antwerp. As a soldier he was able, cruel, and brave. It is interesting to note that Williams frequently refers to him simply by his first name; and the Duke of Alva also, in his correspondence, although he gives other commanders their full name or title, often refers to Romero simply as

Principal Persons Mentioned

Julián. In 1578 he died as a result of a fall from his horse. Thomas Churchyard, *A General Rehearsal of Wars*, f. K4 recto, refers to Romero as a "gallant ancient man of war."

Rouvray

Rouvray appeared in the ranks of the Protestants in the first civil war in France. In 1562 the people of Dieppe gave him the command of a company of cavalry, with which he went to the aid of Rouen. On the return to Dieppe, he drew the Catholics of Arques into an ambuscade at Martin-Église and killed a number of them. Two days later he in turn was ambushed and defeated. He was also involved in several actions subsequently. When the second civil war broke out, Rouvray retired to England, but he soon returned to France and fought courageously and ably on the side of his coreligionists, being entrusted with several important commands. At the conclusion of peace, as is indicated here, he served in Flanders under Ludwig of Nassau. There may actually have been two Huguenot captains named Rouvray. See Eugène Haag, *La France Protestante* (Paris, 1859), IX, 59.

Ruffello. See Barberini

Ruy Gómez de Silva, Prince of Eboli (died 1573)

Gómez had been a childhood friend of Philip II and grew up to be his trusted counselor. As first gentleman of the King's bedchamber, he probably had freer access to the King than anyone. He enjoyed great prestige and power. Gómez was a humane man, well liked by everyone, and seems to have exercised a moderating and kindly influence on Philip II. He often differed violently with Alva.

Ruychaver, Nicolaas (died 1577)

Very little is known about Ruychaver's early life except that he was born at Haarlem. He received a letter of marque from the Prince of Orange in 1569 and became one of the Sea Beggars. He achieved a reputation among that motley throng for his admirable conduct and the justice of his actions. He was present at the capture of Brielle, and after that event he gave up the sea and became a commander in the land forces of the Prince. During 1572 he captured Medemblik, occupied Haarlem for a time, and put

163

down a rebellion at Hoorn. In October, 1573, he took part in the sea battle on the Zuider Zee in which Bossu was taken prisoner, and he was in other actions that same year.

In 1574 he was sent to Antwerp by the Prince to attempt to bring that city over to the side of the States-General, but the Spanish discovered his activities and he narrowly escaped with his life. In 1575–1577 he fought zealously for the Prince in various actions in Holland. In the latter year he took part in the unsuccessful effort to capture Amsterdam, and on the retreat from that action he was murdered by a personal enemy.

Saint Aldegonde. Philips van Marnix, Lord of Saint Aldegonde (1540–1598)

Marnix was a member of a Savoy family that came to the Netherlands with Marguerite of Austria. He studied at Louvain, Paris, and Dôle, and was intended for a religious career. He traveled in Italy and there became not only a humanist but probably a Calvinist. He was an avowed Calvinist as early as 1562. He was among the first members of the League of Nobles and was present when the famous petition was presented to Margaret of Parma by the nobles, April 5, 1566. In 1567 he fled to Germany and was declared banished and his goods confiscated in 1568. He was with the Prince of Orange's army in the campaign in Brabant in 1572. In 1573 he was named Governor of Delft, Schiedam, and Rotterdam, but in November of the same year he fell into the hands of the Spanish at Maaslandsluis. In October of the following year he was exchanged for Mondragón. In 1583 he was the leader in Antwerp when that city was besieged by Parma. After the murder of the Prince of Orange (1584) he became discouraged and retreated to West Souberg and devoted himself to study and writing. He did not sever his connection completely with his old comrades and in 1590 took part in a mission to France and England. He has an important place in history as a writer and is said to be the author of the words of the *Wilhelmus*, the Dutch national anthem.

Saint Luc. François d'Espinay, Seigneur de Saint Luc (1554–1597)

A member of an ancient Norman family, Saint Luc became Governor of Brouage in 1579 and defended it stoutly against the

Principal Persons Mentioned

Huguenots. He was one of the first to recognize Henry IV and served that monarch faithfully. Henry IV gave him the collar of the Order of the Holy Spirit in 1595, and the year following he was named grand master of the artillery. He was a friend of Roger Williams.

Schoonewal. Jonker Jacques Caron, Lord of Schoonewal (died 1573)

Schoonewal was born at Ghent, but very little is known about his early life before 1569, at which date he was captain of a vessel in England in the fleet of the Sea Beggars. He was engaged in various actions in 1569 and 1570, and in these privateering activities he ran afoul of the English government. The Spanish ambassador complained many times about his activities and briefly in 1570 he was imprisoned in England. For a time he succeeded Lumbres as admiral of the Sea Beggars before Lumey had that command. He was present at the capture of Brielle on April 1, 1572, and was killed the following year in an unsuccessful attack by the Sea Beggars on the city of Tholen.

Schouwenburg. Count Joost van Schouwenburg, Lord of Ghemen (ca. 1525–1581)

At the Battle of Heiligerlee, 1568, Schouwenburg was a commander in the forces of the Prince of Orange. Four years later the Prince named him Stadholder of Groningen and Friesland. Subsequently he fled to Germany. He does not appear to have been a particularly admirable character nor to have accomplished a great deal for William of Orange. At the beginning of their association, the Prince noted in a letter to his brother Ludwig that although Schouwenburg had taken an oath of loyalty to Alva he was quite willing to serve the Prince.

Siegen. Hendrik van Siegen

Felix Rachfahl, in his life of William of Orange (The Hague, 1906–1924), III, 429, says that at the Battle of Jemmingen, van Siegen, first lieutenant of Ludwig of Nassau, threw himself into the Ems after the defeat, but that he did not succeed in getting away and was captured by the Spanish, as was mentioned by Alva.

Smith, Captain

Williams says that most of the captains he mentions at this point in the text were present at the siege of Haarlem. In the *Comentario de Coronel Francisco Verdugo* (Madrid, 1872), p. 47, the author says, "Inside was Colonel Smith, a Scot, and in my [Verdugo's] regiment there was a Captain Hamilton. Hamilton told Smith that he would be rescued and that he [Hamilton] would be there in two days. . . . Captain Caniga, who heard them speaking, though he did not completely understand the language, said that he thought they were exchanging messages, . . . and since I could not prove what they were saying and I was suspicious, I looked for some excuse to remove Hamilton from my regiment, and I did so."

Steinbach. Captain Jacob von Steinbach

Steinbach was second in command of a regiment of German mercenaries commanded by Lazarus Muller which had been recruited by Sonoy at Bremen and Hamburg in May, 1572. He succeeded to the command of the regiment in June of the same year. He was one of the defenders of Haarlem and one of the handful of German commanders who were not executed by the Spanish at the fall of Haarlem. Subsequent to that catastrophe he served with part of his regiment in the Spanish forces for a time. Some years afterward, in 1577, he offered the services of himself and his troops to Queen Elizabeth on moderate terms for as long as the Queen pleased (*Calendar of State Papers, Foreign, 1577–1578,* p. 6). In 1578 he was again in the service of the States, and he took part in 1579 in the defense of upper Gelderland. In the latter part of that year he and his troops, being unpaid, went on a plundering expedition around Lingen (Ten Raa and Bas, I, 53).

Treslong, see Blois

Tseraerts. Jerome Tseraerts (ca. 1540–1573)

Tseraerts was a Brabant nobleman who had served the Prince of Orange as master of the horse. He took part in the Compromise and accompanied the Prince of Orange to Dillenburg in 1567. In February, 1568, he was sent to England by the Prince to place the case of the insurgents before Queen Elizabeth. In April of the same year he returned to the Netherlands and took part in the campaigns of 1568. In 1569 he was again in England, where he took command of one of the ships of the Sea Beggars under Lumbres. After the capture of Brielle he arrived with seven ships off Walcheren and was soon after named Governor of that island. His attempts to seize Brugge and Goes miscarried. He later took part in the effort to relieve Haarlem and was wounded in that action. As Governor of Gertruidenberg he was able to prevent an outbreak of iconoclasm but was killed there in a revolt in September, 1573. He was an upright and trustworthy man, but there were frequent complaints about his crudity and lack of administrative ability.

Valdéz. Francisco de Valdéz (died ca. 1580)

Valdéz began his military career under the Emperor Charles V. He served in the Schmalkaldic war in 1546 and in Africa in 1550. He came to the Netherlands with Alva. He served as *sargento mayor* and wrote a book on the functions of that post, *Dialogo militar . . . en el qual se trata del oficio del sargento mayor* (Madrid, 1590), which was translated into both English and Italian. He took part in the Battle of Mook. At the siege of Leiden, 1573–1574, Valdéz was a *maestre de campo* and conducted the siege with skill and competence; but when the Spanish failed to take the city, the soldiery, disappointed in their expectations of plunder, turned against Valdéz and several times held him prisoner. During the siege, Valdéz courted a maiden in The Hague nearby whom he later married. In 1579 he took part in the siege of Maastricht. He died at Antwerp about 1580. In addition to the work already mentioned, he wrote *Espeio, y deceplina militar* (Brussels, 1589).

Verdugo. Francisco Verdugo (1536–1597)

Verdugo began his military career at the age of eighteen and displayed outstanding ability at the Battle of Saint-Quentin. On the orders of Margaret of Parma, Verdugo recruited troops to put down the first outbreaks of iconoclasm. He served under Cristóbal Mondragón and was named sergeant major of the army in the Netherlands under the Duke of Alva. He fought in Groningen at the siege of Haarlem, in many actions up to and including Gembloux, and numerous actions after that. Juan Bautista de Tassis, Williams' doughty antagonist, was his lieutenant. He was still fighting (this time the French) in the year of his death. He is the

Principal Persons Mentioned

author of a book on the wars in the Low Countries entitled *Comentario del Coronel Francisco Verdugo,* first printed at Naples in 1610.

Vitelli. Chiappino Vitelli, Marquis of Cetona (1520–1576)

Vitelli was a well-known Florentine nobleman. In his early years he fought for Grand Duke Cosimo de' Medici in the war with Siena. In 1564 he was a commander in the forces which Philip II of Spain sent to Africa to fight the Moors. He came to the Netherlands with Alva, was at the Battle of Jemmingen, and fought elsewhere in Friesland in 1568. In 1569 he accompanied Barberini (*q.v.*) on a mission to England. He was at the siege of Mons and had an important part in the defeat of the French forces under Genlis (*q.v.*). In subsequent years he took part in many important actions. He was at the siege of Zierikzee in 1576. At that time he was so exceessively fat that he used a sedan chair and had the misfortune to fall out of it. He was injured and died soon afterward.

Walsingham. Sir Francis Walsingham (1530?–1590)

Walsingham entered Parliament in 1559. Later he was engaged in the task of gathering information on foreign governments for his own government. Many of the letters from his spies and informants in the Low Countries are included in the *Calendar of State Papers.* He favored intervention in the Netherlands on behalf of the Prince of Orange and the States-General. The standard biography is Conyers Read, *Mr. Secretary Walsingham and the Policy of Queen Elizabeth* (Oxford, 1925).

Worst. Ewout Pietersz. Worst

Louis du Gardin wrote of Worst, June 9, 1572 (*Archives . . . de la Maison d'Orange-Nassau,* 1st ser., III, 436), that "Captain Worst of Flushing has performed marvelous feats of war." This statement was no exaggeration, for a number of times he engaged far superior fleets and came off victorious. For example, Le Petit notes that on one occasion with seven ships he defeated an enemy fleet of thirty.

Emanuel van Meteren, *L'histoire des Pays-Bas* (The Hague, 1618), f. 72 verso, says that Worst obtained powder, arms, supplies, and ships for the Flushingers through a relative at Antwerp, that he was valiant, and that the Flushingers named him admiral in recognition of his services. Van Meteren goes on to say (f. 86 verso) that he was able, honest, and experienced, and that he was above all hardy, resolute, diligent, sincere, and feared by the Spanish. Concerning his death in 1572, Le Petit wrote (*La grande chronique*, p. 249) that "at this time died the Captain Thibaut Worst, Admiral of Flushing, a captain who was as far removed from ambition and avarice as he was valiant and hardy."

Yorke, or York, Rowland (died 1588)

Yorke was in the band of volunteers which went to the Netherlands in 1572 with Thomas Morgan, and he took part in Sir Humphrey Gilbert's attack on Goes. Since he was a Roman Catholic, he was distrusted by the States, and their distrust was eventually justified. In 1584 he was detected in a plot to betray Ghent to the Duke of Parma. He was taken as a prisoner to Brussels but was freed at the request of Parma. Thereafter he served Parma for a time, but he returned to England and then took service under Sidney in the Netherlands.

A few years later, having been appointed to the command of the Zutphen sconce, he betrayed that strong point to the Spanish and induced Sir William Stanley to do the same for Deventer. He changed sides in the Netherlands struggle and eventually became captain of a troop of lancers in the Spanish forces. Yet he did not remain loyal to the Spanish. He died in 1588. Following a decision of a military court martial, his body was disinterred and hanged in 1591 by order of the States' government.